OUR HEAVENLY FATHER

OUR HEAVENLY FATHER

A STUDY OF THE NATURE
AND DOCTRINE OF GOD

BY THE
REV. PETER GREEN, M.A.

CANON OF MANCHESTER
CHAPLAIN TO H.M. THE KING

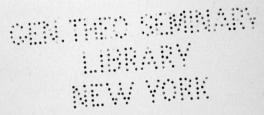
LONGMANS GREEN, AND CO.
LONDON | NEW YORK | TORONTO
1930

LONGMANS, GREEN AND CO. LTD.

39 PATERNOSTER ROW, LONDON, E.C.4
6 OLD COURT HOUSE STREET, CALCUTTA
53 NICOL ROAD, BOMBAY
MOUNT ROAD, MADRAS

LONGMANS, GREEN AND CO.

55 FIFTH AVENUE, NEW YORK
221 EAST 20TH STREET, CHICAGO
TREMONT TEMPLE, BOSTON
128-132 UNIVERSITY AVENUE, TORONTO

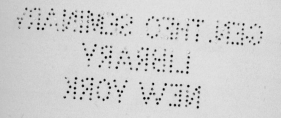

Made in Great Britain

PREFACE

THIS book is in the nature of a sequel to my earlier book, *Our Lord and Saviour*. The object of that book was stated to be " to help those who desire a more personal relationship to Christ than they have yet enjoyed." It would, therefore, seem right that it should have a sequel, *Our Heavenly Father*. For it is the function of Christ to reveal the Father, and "no man knoweth the Father, save the Son, and he to whomsoever the Son will reveal Him." [1]

But this book is not merely a sequel. It is inspired by an independent conviction; the conviction that the chief feature of our age is its deep godlessness. Many people, no doubt, will be annoyed and offended by that statement. They will point to the greater orderliness, kindliness, and sobriety of the mass of the nation; to the growing tenderness of the public conscience in the matter of injustice or cruelty to men and to animals; to higher standards of conduct alike in public and private life. All these things may be, and doubtless are, true. But they are irrelevant. I am not discussing morality or civilization. When I said godlessness, I meant godlessness. I meant that increasing numbers of people are allowing God to pass altogether out of their lives. " God is not in all their thoughts." [2] And many are content that it should be so. On the day on which this preface was written the morning papers reported a well-known politician, speaking on the alleged failure of Christianity, as declaring his belief that Christianity could never regain its power, but that the religion of the future would concern itself only with conduct, with personal morality, and with the service of one's fellow-men. If the idea of a spiritual Being, external to the world, occupied any place in men's minds, which he regarded as unlikely, it would be a purely private and personal matter. To one

[1] Matt. xi. 27.   [2] Psalm x. 4.

who believes that the knowledge and love of God is not merely the best thing in life, but, in a very real sense, life itself, and who regards religion as the root from which personal morality and the spirit of social service spring as flowers, such a view appears dreary and Philistine, incredible and unattractive, to the last degree. What the world needs is a great return to God, and such a return alone can save the individual from misery and society from collapse. The object, then, of this book is to recall men to " the practice of the presence of God."

Unfortunately, the present book has not proved anything like as easy to write as the earlier one, and will not, I fear, be found as easy to read. In writing about Jesus there was no need for argument. I had not even to paint a picture. All that was necessary was to suggest paths which my readers might tread for themselves, and which would, I believed, lead them to a vision of Him. But in writing of God one has to be constantly arguing, since the world is full of false ideas about Him. Indeed, I have hardly been able to make a single statement about God without turning aside to meet some criticism or to discuss some denial. This has given, I fear, a haphazard appearance to the book. Yet it is not without a plan, and it may help the reader to understand the book if I briefly outline that plan.

Chapter I defines religion as a disinterested delight in God for His own sake.

Chapter II discusses the objections brought against this definition by those who deny that religion is chiefly concerned with " a hypothetical Being beyond the skies," and assert that true religion is concerned chiefly with being good (morality) and doing good (service).

Chapter III meets another class of objections to our definition based on the widespread agnosticism of our day, an agnosticism which remains as an evil legacy from the last half of the nineteenth century.

In Chapter IV I get back to the main line of my argument, and try to describe what God is found to be like when we actually know Him. The title of the chapter might well have been : " What we find God to be when we know Him."

In Chapters V and VI I have again to discuss objections. The picture I have tried to paint of God in Chapter IV will make some people ask : " But can such a God be reconciled with the teachings of modern science as to Natural Law ? " So I have had to discuss " Divine Providence, Prayer and Miracle." Again, others will ask : " How can your picture of God be reconciled with the existence, in this world, of sin and pain ? " So I have had to examine, very briefly, the Problem of Pain.

In Chapter VII I return again to the main line of my argument, and try to state—it is impossible to do more than state—the Church's doctrine of God, the doctrine of the Blessed Trinity.

In Chapter VIII I have attempted a brief sketch of what can only be called Christian Cosmology. I am convinced that the immense increase in all branches of human knowledge, and the lack, on the part of the Church, of any authoritative teaching, together with the chaos of opinions, assertions, denials, and questionings which confronts us in the popular Press, combine to leave ordinary men and women in a state of bewilderment. They want a *weltanschauung*, a mental picture, of what they may believe about God, and Man, and the Universe. And so Chapter VIII is a brief, and necessarily bald and dogmatic, statement of what I believe. Readers will, no doubt, modify it for themselves. But I cannot think that it is far from the truth. I find it good for thought and for practice, good to think by and to live by.

CONTENTS

" The presence of evil amongst us and in us, in its manifold forms of suffering and selfishness and loss and crime, is a reality which no ingenuity can hide or dissemble. Revelation did not cause this terrible affliction, but it shows that it does not belong to the essence of creation or to the essence of man. It shows, therefore that it is remediable : that it can be removed from man without destroying his true nature, nay, rather that his true nature is vindicated by the removal. The idea of Christ's sufferings, the idea of redemption, presupposes the idea of a Fall. Such an idea is, I will venture to say, a necessary condition of human hope. No view of life can be so inexpressibly sad as that which denies the Fall."

The Historic Faith, by BISHOP B. F. WESTCOTT.

CHAPTER I

OUR topic, in this book, is God. Our task will be to learn what we can of His nature, of His attitude towards men, and of their right attitude towards Him. We shall try to discover how best we can come to a fuller knowledge of God, and shall seek to understand what are the results, on the whole of a man's life and character, of knowing and loving God.

And no subject, surely, could be of greater interest or importance. For clearly either God exists and may be known, or else He does not exist, and the atheist is right in denying that there is any such Being. The third alternative, namely, that He exists, but cannot be known by man, we can unhesitatingly reject. For, as we shall see in a later chapter, any Being to whom it could be worth while to give the name of God must desire to reveal Himself to His creatures and to earn their love. So then the subject of God is one of intense interest and importance, a subject which no man can afford to ignore. The man who " says in his heart ' There is no God,' " is branded by the psalmist as a fool.[1] But more foolish still is the man who believes that there is a God, and who would indignantly deny that he was an atheist, yet who, when it comes to the active practice of religious duties and observances, is content to say : " Oh ! I never bother." Yet we all know such men, and meet them everywhere, every day, in every rank and station of life.

For religion, of which any number of definitions have been offered, may best be defined, by a religious man, as *a disinterested delight in God for His own sake*. I say that it may best be defined in these words, " by a religious man."

---

[1] Ps. xiv. 1 and liii. 1.

The philosopher, the man of science, the historian may each find some other definition more convenient, for each will, naturally and rightly, concentrate his attention on those aspects of his subject which specially concern him. But when we, as religious men and women, do the same, concentrating on those aspects of religion that specially concern us, and trying to separate the essential from the unessential, we shall, I am convinced, find no better definition of religion than that it is a disinterested delight in God for His own sake.

This, of course, is what is implied in the Fourth Gospel, where we read : " This is life eternal, that they might know Thee, the only true God, and Jesus Christ, Whom Thou hast sent."[2] The knowledge of God is not one of the good things in life. It is not even the best thing in life. It is life itself. It makes all other goods possible. God is our Sun ; and as all the glories of a landscape, the brightness of the sky, the colours of the flowers, the innumerable tints of the whole picture, are derived from the sun, and are lost in one common darkness when the sun sets, so all good things which man can enjoy, all goodness, truth, and beauty, are, even if we do not know it, no more than reflected rays of His brightness.

To define religion thus, as a disinterested delight in God for His own sake, has another advantage besides that of being in agreement with the teaching of Holy Scripture. It brings religion into line with all the other great activities of the human mind. The true artist is the man who loves beauty for its own sake. If you were to ask him what was the practical use of his symphony, his poem, or his picture, he would turn from you as from a Philistine unworthy of a moment's attention. Modern science has achieved wonders of practical utility, and yielded a thousand comforts and conveniences for man's daily use. But the true man of science desires knowledge for its own sake. If you were to ask the astronomer what ends of practical utility were served by finding out the internal temperature of Sirius or the diameter of Antares, he would probably be the first to admit that such knowledge has no commercial value,

[2] John xvii. 3.

and may well never prove of use in the daily affairs of men.
But he would turn from your silly questions undisturbed
and address himself, with undiminished enthusiasm, to his
observations and calculations. The truly moral man does
not love goodness because, trusting in the maxim that
" Honesty is the best policy," he hopes to benefit by it ;
nor because a truthful lad makes a more satisfactory office-
boy than an untruthful one. He does not hate vice merely
because drunkenness and lust break up homes, and lower
the nation's annual output of wealth. No indeed ! He
loves goodness for its own sake. He cries : *Fiat justitia,
ruat cœlum—Let the right be done though the heavens fall.*
For Beauty, Truth, and Goodness are to be sought for their
own sakes ; and those who love them do so with a disinterested love which takes no account of self.

How much more is this the case when all Beauty, Truth,
and Goodness are sought not singly, but in one supreme
goal ; not faintly shadowed forth in broken rays, but
embodied in a Personal Being, in God our Heavenly Father.
All true love is selfless, and the measure of love is the measure
of its disinterestedness. This Blake knew when he wrote :

> Love seeketh not itself to please,
>   Nor for itself hath any care,
> But for another gives its ease,
>   And builds a heaven in hell's despair.

And what is true of the noblest human love, at its highest
and best, must be supremely true of Divine love. Religion
must be a disinterested delight in God for His own sake.
How wisely Dr. Inge speaks when he says of " the truly
religious man " that " in his intense desire for the
purification of his motives he almost wishes that Heaven
and Hell were blotted out, that he might serve God for
Himself alone." [3]

I sometimes think that one reason why there was no
widespread revival of religion in the early days after the
War was just because men sought Him, often quite sincerely,

---

[3] *Light, Life, and Love : Selections from the German Mystics of the
Middle Ages*, p. xlvi.   Methuen & Co.   1904.

for His gifts rather than for Himself. Many of our leaders, in Church and State, were forward in pointing out that we should not rebuild Europe, nor repair the ravages of the War, without " spiritual sanctions." Which was only another way of saying that we should achieve nothing without God's help. But profoundly true as this was, the emphasis often seemed wrongly laid on our need rather than on God's glory. So much stress was laid on our wants and difficulties, and on the importance of getting God to help us to put things right, that it often sounded as if a religious revival meant a summons to God to come and make Himself useful. It was almost as if we were calling to God to join a Ministry of Reconstruction, and trying to co-opt Him on to our General Purposes Committee at the Town Hall. But there is no single fact connected with religion of which I am more deeply convinced than this, namely, that God will never come into our lives, nor into the life of a nation, as a kind of general servant. If He comes at all He must come as Master. I once heard an old Wesleyan local preacher, at an open-air service, give beautiful expression to this truth. " God," he declared, " is the best Master in the world ; but He will *be* Master." Wherever He comes He comes to bless. But where men desire His blessings more than they desire Him Himself He does not come at all. When I was a little boy, taken to church by my parents, I did not like the second commandment. *For I the Lord thy God am a jealous God.* I used to wonder why people said such horrid things about God. But now I know that the commandment speaks the truth. God is jealous over us with a divine jealousy. He is not willing that anything should occupy in our hearts the place which belongs to Him. God is so good, His nature is so wholly and exclusively love, that if there were anything that could make us happier than the knowledge and love of Him, if there were anything which could satisfy man's nature apart from Him, He would be willing that we should forget Him. But that is impossible, for what St. Augustine says of God is true : " Thou hast made us for Thyself, and our heart is restless till it rests in Thee." [4]

[4] *Confessions*, Bk. I., chapter i.

So then the man who desires good must desire God. And the man who desires God must desire Him for His own sake. For, indeed, God has nothing to give to the soul but Himself :

> Then rest my long-divided heart,
>   Fixed on this blissful centre, rest ;
> Nor ever from my Lord depart,
>   With Him of every good possessed.[5]

I do not think that anyone can deny that there is very real danger lest men should desire God's gifts instead of Him, and measure the value of religion by the amount of moral, social, and even economic fruit that it yields. Indeed, many people to-day go further still and seem to see something particularly noble and attractive in the attitude towards life which ignores God altogether. They set their affections on things on the earth, not on things above,[6] and appear to consider such behaviour a proof of their wisdom. I do not want to appear to exaggerate. I don't want to seem to rail without cause at present-day religious tendencies in England. What I am complaining of is so common that, like many other things that we see daily, it escapes our attention. So I will quote a very typical example, and I expect that every reader will be able to recall similar experiences of his own. Soon after the War I was chairman at a bazaar which was opened by a prominent member of Parliament. When the opening ceremony was ended something, I cannot imagine what, moved him to expound, for my benefit, what he called his religion. He was not, he declared, a member of any denomination or sect, and he felt no call to attend public worship. Doctrines, creeds, and dogmas did not interest him. Religion for him had nothing to do with a far-off heaven, or with a mysterious Being beyond the skies. His religion was a " Here-and-now" religion. To make every one happy all round him, and to leave the world better than he found it, was, he assured me,

[5] The hymn, " O happy day that fixed my choice," by P. Doddridge, 1702–1751.
[6] Col. iii. 2.

his religion. He evidently thought, poor man, that he was presenting himself to me in a very noble and attractive light, and had no idea of the half comic, half tragic mixture of contempt and despair with which I listened. Man's highest good, that for which the saints and sages of all time have hungered and thirsted, that for which God-intoxicated men have given up all else and counted their loss gain, all this meant nothing to him. But this was the least part of his offence. He not only could see nothing in God to desire ; he claimed my admiration and applause, because he was so blind, so spiritually stunted. It was as if he had turned from a Beethoven symphony to express his preference for the latest example of vulgar, ear-splitting jazz, and had invited me to praise his musical taste and discernment. It was as if he had ranked a smudgy picture from the *Police Gazette* above an Albrecht Dürer print, and had, in the same breath, claimed my admiration for his ability as an art critic. If St. Augustine's description of the human heart, quoted above, is correct, how dead, how far gone from its true purpose and end, must a heart be which can not only rest wholly content without God, but actually deems such a condition a happy one ! One can forgive a mere lad for excusing his neglect of religion by declaring that, after a week of hard work in the office or the factory, a day in the fresh air " does him more good " than attendance at a place of worship, for he is young and un-developed, with the powers of mind and spirit still largely unawakened. But surely no adult, no one who claims to be a grown man or woman, should talk as if every faculty in man were worth cultivating except the soul, and every good worth striving for except God. And even in the mouth of a lad such a way of speaking is not pleasant. The name by which we have all been taught to speak of God, since the days when we first learned to say our prayers at our mothers' knee, the name *Our Father*, should teach us better. What young man, rebuked for neglecting his aged parents, would care to reply : " Oh ! it does me more good to play a round of golf, or to spend an hour at billiards, than to talk to a couple of old invalids in a stuffy room ? " Or to draw an illustration from the other highest and most

sacred relation between one human being and another—
and all the beautiful and sacred relations between human
beings are but faint shadows and types of the relation of
the soul to God—how would it sound if a young man were
to declare that when he went courting he would look for
nothing but a good cook, since a well-planned and prepared
meal would " do him more good " than mere beauty of
face, refinement of mind, or nobility of spirit in his life's
partner ?

I expect by now I shall have alienated the sympathies of
many, perhaps of most, of my readers. I shall be told that
I am falling into the common parsonic habit of identifying
an interest in, and taste for, church-going with religion.
I shall be assured that the people who attend no place of
worship, and make no profession of religion, are often more
truly religious, more interested in God, than the practising
members of the various denominations. Yes, I shall be
told this. But I shall not believe it. The newspapers daily
repeat the assertion ; but they do it because it flatters the
self-esteem of their readers. When a man, after breakfast
on Sunday morning, in the intervals of smoking a pipe and
reading his morning paper, debates whether to go to church
or to spend the time till the public-houses open resting,
gardening, or playing golf, nothing is more soothing than
to be assured that if he pleases himself, and neglects God,
he is really more truly religious than his neighbour who is
to be found Sunday by Sunday in his place at church. But
the fact that he can and does believe such nonsense is
merely a saddening proof of man's powers of self-deception.
We are often told that the man in the street is really
religious, and desires the knowledge of God and His service,
but finds nothing in the services offered to him by the
churches and chapels which satisfies his longings. But
how strange this is ! Here is Mr. John Smith athirst for
God, yet all the religious denominations from Rome to
Geneva, all the Roman Catholics, Anglicans, Presbyterians,
Baptists, Congregationalists, Wesleyans, Quakers, Unitar-
ians, Bible Christians, Christian Scientists, Theosophists,
and the rest of them, can devise nothing in the way of
worship which will meet :

His spirit's strange deep longings,
Interpreting its need.

He has, at least in every town of any size, every type of
worship from the gorgeous splendour of a High Mass to
the simple warmth and brotherliness of Primitive Methodist
worship ; from the stately dignity of an Anglican cathedral
to the intense silence and spiritual quiet of a Quaker meeting.
But none have any power to appeal to him, so the poor
fellow has to spend Sunday morning in bed with the news-
paper, the afternoon pottering about with his fowls in the
backyard, and the evening visiting friends. Let us try to
be realists, and to face facts. If a man were to declare that
he was profoundly musical, with a passionate love of the
best music and an understanding of it far truer than that of
most musical people, what should we say to him if he went
on to say that he had not crossed the threshold of a concert
hall for years ? Let us suppose that he finds the Queen's
Hall Symphony Concerts too severely classical, a string
quartette too dull, the opera too conventional, Gilbert and
Sullivan too popular, a military band too glaring, a solo
pianist lacking in interest ; let us imagine him declaring his
dislike for vocal music, and his inability to keep awake
during concerted instrumental pieces ; let us hear him
admit that classical music sends him to sleep and a jazz
band gives him a headache. How shall we meet his claims
to be profoundly musical ? What shall we say when he
declares that he has more real love for, and understanding
of, music than many men and women who never miss a
concert if they can help it ? Shall we not say : " My dear
friend, you deceive yourself. You are *not* musical at all.
It is, of course, possible that you have natural powers
which, properly cultivated, might have made you a fine,
even a great musician. But if that is so you have allowed
them to become atrophied by long neglect. It flatters
your self-esteem to talk about your taste for music, and
you have been doing so for so long that friends and neighbours have been taken in by your talk, and have fallen into
the silly habit of saying : ' How musical Mr. Smith is !
Much more truly musical than many who play, and sing,

and spend a fortune on concert tickets.' But you are a fraud. To-day you have no real love for music at all." And if we should feel justified in speaking thus plainly when a love for music is concerned, ought we to speak less plainly when love of God is the point at issue ? St. Paul tells us that the truth should be spoken " in love."[7] Certainly it is important that it should be spoken in love, since angry railing effects nothing. But it is not less important that it should be spoken, and spoken clearly. The first duty of the Church to-day is to say to the many thousands of her children who neglect every ordinance of religion : " It is not true that you are deeply religious. You have no taste for God. No doubt you, like all other human beings, are stirred from time to time by vague religious emotions, but they never find expression in any actions and so they come to nothing. Your so-called religion costs you nothing in effort or self-sacrifice. It costs you nothing and it is worth what it costs you." For the Church to speak in this way, clearly, consistently, and at all times, would be the truest kindness, for many thousands of people in England are sunk in blind self-deception and self-satisfaction. Believing themselves to be everything that God must approve and man should applaud, they are allowing all the powers of the soul to atrophy, and are losing the best thing in life, the knowledge and love of God.

If we ask the reason for this strange neglect of God, this tragic alienation of thousands from the true purpose and end of their being, we may find it, I think, in two closely-allied causes. I do not speak here of sin, for I am not thinking of those people whom the world calls sinners, the vicious, the drunken, the dishonest. No, I am thinking of the pleasant, respectable, neighbourly people, the good parents, the upright business men, the friendly neighbours, who are nevertheless sunk in worldliness, and of whom it becomes daily more and more true that " neither is God in all his thoughts."[8] Two things seem chiefly responsible for this condition of things. The first is the fierce struggle for wealth. Our whole life is organized on a basis which makes money the chief aim. If it were possible so to recast

[7] Eph. iv. 15.   [8] Ps. x. 4.

society, and so to redirect man's desires, that "having food and raiment"[9] we might be therewith content, men would be free to find the true interest and occupation of their lives in knowledge, beauty, goodness, friendship, service, and that to which all these things lead, and in which they all find their perfection, namely, God. But our Saviour's words are true: "Ye cannot serve God and mammon."[10] To say this is not to say that it is impossible to love and serve God in modern society; nor is it to say that rich people are any farther off from God than poor people. A poor man, struggling to get on and with his whole outlook on life ordered on what one may call a cash basis, *may be* more worldly than a millionaire. A millionaire, living surrounded by every modern luxury and refinement, *may be* divorced from the world and be living a life rooted and grounded in God. For the soul's life is choked by the "cares" as well as the "riches and pleasures of this life,"[11] and the mischief is not in the things themselves, but in a heart set on them. Rich and poor alike are in danger, and rich and poor can recognize the danger, and strive against it. But it cannot be denied that in what Mr. Tawney has so well named an *acquisitive society* the danger of God being forgotten is great. His place in our hearts is taken by other gods, and our lives are ruled and our standards of judgment determined by other laws than His.

And the other cause for the growing godlessness of the modern world is due to the noise, hurry, and racket of our lives.

> The world is too much with us; late and soon,
> Getting and spending, we lay waste our powers.

Most of us live in the shallows. We neither think deeply nor feel deeply. We read more books than we remember, and hear more talk than we can take in, and see more pictures than we can study or appreciate; and we do it all with little mental effort, little response, on our part, of vital interest or sympathy. Experiences may be said

[9] 1 Tim vi. 8.   [10] Luke xvi. 13.
[11] Luke viii. 14.

rather to pass over our minds than to enter into them. And the result is mental and spiritual shallowness. Some time ago I heard a public speaker say that if a man could spend five years on a desert island, and each New Year's Day were given one really great book, which he would read and re-read and think about and make his own, he would at the end be a better educated man than many who had raced through a book a day for half a century. But there is nothing on which the prevailing shallowness of the present age has a more disastrous effect than on religion. God does not meet with us in the shallows of our nature. He meets us, if at all, in the deep places of personality, in times of profound thought, of intense feeling, of high and testing resolve. The true Israel, the man who as a prince has power with God, and with men, and who prevails,[12] is the man who has said to God :

> Come, O Thou Traveller unknown,
> Whom still I hold, but cannot see,
> My company before is gone,
> And I am left alone with Thee ;
> With Thee all night I mean to stay,
> And wrestle till the break of day.

For religion, as I have said, is a disinterested delight in God for His own sake ; and in man's life God is the " one thing needful." And the deep-seated sickness of our modern life is neglect of God. Many people, many really good and excellent people, are " careful and troubled about many things," but " one thing is needful,"[13] the knowledge and love of God, and lack of God in the lives of thousands of men and women is the deep-seated cause of most of our ills. If, like the man in Stevenson's fable,[14] we had the clear-shining touchstone of truth, and could turn it on the men we meet daily, of how many should we have to say that " his soul was shrunk into the smallness of a pea, and his heart was a bag of little fears like scorpions, and love was dead in his bosom " ? Not of all, thank God !

[12] Gen. xxxii. 28. [13] Luke x. 41 and 42.
[14] *Fables*, by R. L. Stevenson, " The Touchstone."

Perhaps not of as many as we are sometimes tempted to think.

As I shall have much to criticise in the religion of England to-day, it is necessary to give this caution. We none of us can look into another's heart, and with people as naturally reticent on religious matters as English people are, we do well to remind ourselves that there is more true religion than we see, or know about. I am not now taking refuge in the shallow optimism which I have myself just condemned; the shallow optimism which declares that, provided a man lives a fairly decent life, and is pleasant in the home, and popular at his club, he is to be ranked a Christian, called religious, and regarded as satisfying all reasonable requirements of man and God. I mean that there must be many more men and women than we know of who really love God; men and women in whose lives God counts for something; souls in which a disinterested delight in Him for His own sake glows and burns.

There is a story which illustrates my meaning, and which may help others, as it has often helped me. One Monday, more than twenty years ago, I was walking, between twelve and one o'clock, in a particularly unlovely suburb of Manchester. For some reason, I forget why, I was very much depressed. I felt that

> My warnings fray
> No one, and no one they convert,
> And no one helps me to assert
> How hard it is to really be
> A Christian.

I was passing a bare open space, near a great ironworks, and some two hundred men and lads, out for their dinner-hour, were kicking footballs about. I looked at them, wondering why the Church so failed to win men to God, and what one could do to awaken religion in men and lads like these. Suddenly a football bounded almost to my feet, and a boy of nineteen in blue-cotton trousers followed it and, picking it up, kicked it back to his mates. As he did so he smiled at me, and I saw he was the lad who had served me that morning at the half-past seven celebration

of Holy Communion. In those days ironworkers started
at six a.m. every day except Monday, when the hour was
nine a.m.. Yet Johnny, who had to leave home at five-
thirty a.m. on ordinary days to get to work, gave up one
Monday a fortnight to serve at seven-thirty a.m., from the
time he left school till he married. And one day he said to
me, after serving : " It was beautiful in church to-day.
I wish I could serve every day." What did the boy find
beautiful in a dark, cold, dingy city church at eight
o'clock on a drizzling November morning in Salford ?
No mere outward beauty, I am sure. Very early in life
Johnny could have made his own the words of the
psalmist :

> One thing have I desired of the Lord, which I will require ;
> even that I may dwell in the house of the Lord all the days
> of my life, to behold the fair beauty of the Lord, and to
> visit His temple.[15]

And there I had been, a few moments before, looking on
those two hundred men and lads, and doubting whether
any of them knew or loved God ! No doubt some of them
were unawakened. But surely there could also be little doubt
that there were others like Johnny ; boys and men who
served with joy at altars, Anglican or Roman, or who taught
in Sunday Schools and Ragged Schools, or preached in the
street for the Wesleyans or the Salvation Army. We do
well, when we are tempted to give way to depression, to
remember God's hidden saints. For the man or woman
who sits next you in a tram, or jostles you in a crowded
street, or serves you in a shop, may have the love of God
burning in his or her heart, like a fire. There are times
when we all fall into unhappiness and are tempted to forget
that just as many whom we meet know nothing of our
inward experiences of God, our secret consolations in Christ,
so there must be many among those we meet casually day
by day who also have a secret love of God alight in them,
ready to blaze out as occasion offers, of which we, in turn,
are ignorant.

[15] Ps. xxvii. 4.   P.B. version.

And yet I know that it is true.
  Oh light a flame within my heart,
That I may love Thee more and more,
  Until I see Thee as Thou art.

In the next chapter I shall have to answer a criticism which, I expect, has suggested itself to many of my readers by now.

CHAPTER II

As I said at the end of the last chapter, I must now prepare to meet a criticism which will probably have suggested itself to the minds of the majority of my readers. I cannot doubt that, in the true scriptural sense of the word, I shall have *offended*, that is to say puzzled, weakened, and alienated, some people by my criticism of the member of Parliament who boasted of having no interest in " a far-off Heaven or a mysterious Being beyond the skies," and who claimed to possess a " here-and-now " religion which aimed only at making everybody round him happy and leaving the world better than he found it. Some, at least, perhaps many, of my readers, especially among generous-hearted young people of both sexes, will feel inclined to exclaim : " Well, anyhow, that is the sort of man I admire. That is the only sort of religion for which I have any use." And will they not be right ? Is not the plain man, who may not be much of a church-goer and who, perhaps, does not even say his prayers, but who lives an upright life and tries to do what good he can, more truly religious than many a man whose eyes are set on Heaven ?

It is certainly with no desire to belittle or underrate either morality (the living of a pure and upright life) or benevolence (the seeking to make others happy and to do what good one can) that I shall assert that a man may lead a life of the highest and most austere morality, and may spend all his days in the service of his fellow-men, and may yet be, in the truest sense of the word, profoundly irreligious. If this offends the reader, I shall beg him to pause and consider most earnestly—yes, and most prayerfully—exactly what his attitude implies. What really does it amount to when a man declares that morality and

philanthropy are enough, and that the man who displays these virtues has all that we have any right to
demand of anyone ? It amounts to this, that we find ourselves saying, not perhaps in words, but quite plainly by
implication :

> " I do think a man's character matters."
> " I do think the happiness and well-being of my
> fellow-creatures, and of society, matters."
> " I do not think God matters."

But thus to put our comfort and present happiness, or the
welfare and progress of society, before the glory of God is
to fall into the sin so strongly condemned by St. Paul when
he speaks of those " who changed the truth of God into a
lie, and worshipped and served the creature more than the
Creator, Who is blessed for evermore."[1] I do not think it
would be difficult to prove from history that the result of
forgetting God is always the same, the fearful moral corruption of society. For, apart from God, and from belief
that man is made in His image, there seems to me to be
no foundation for morals, no sure basis for distinctions of
right and wrong. But the subject of God and morals is
one we shall have to come back to in a later chapter.[2]
All I want to say here and now is that neither morality,
nor philanthropy, nor both together are true religion, nor
an adequate substitute for it.

I am not suggesting that a man can truly delight in
God for His own sake without striving both to live a good
life and to serve his fellow-men. Indeed, it is obvious that,
if my definition is right, true religion cannot exist apart
from morality and philanthropy. For no man can delight
in a God of Whom he has had no vision at any time : yet
without holiness no man shall see the Lord.[3] And no man
can love his fellow-men without desiring to serve them :
for " he that loveth not his brother whom he hath seen,
how can he love God Whom he hath not seen ? " So we
need not discuss the question whether religion without
either morality or love of one's fellows is worth having.

---

[1] Romans i. 25.   [2] Chapter IV.   [3] Heb. xii. 14.

We shall simply deny that any such thing can exist. But morality and philanthropy clearly can and do exist without love for, or interest in, God. And this we shall deplore, and we shall assert that no purity of life and no devotion to the service of humanity can compensate man for the lack of that which is his highest good, namely, conscious communion with God. And in saying this we have on our side the authority of Jesus. Asked as to which was the chief commandment of the Law, He replied : " The first of all the commandments is ' Hear, O Israel, The Lord our God is one Lord ; And thou shalt love the Lord thy God with all thy heart, and with all thy soul, and with all thy mind, and with all thy strength ' : this is the first commandment." [4] The second : " Thou shalt love thy neighbour as thyself," is *like* it ; as the reflection of the sun in a lake is like the sun, or the image of a man in a mirror is like the man. But the reality in these two cases is the sun, or the man ; the reflection is but an image, something derived from, and dependent on, the reality.

Now, curiously enough, this is exactly the position taken up in that text from the Epistle of St. James which is so often quoted as if it denied the necessity of absorption in God. S. T. Coleridge was right when he said, in his *Aids to Reflection* : " I need not inform the religious reader that James, chapter i, verse 27, [5] is the favourite text and most boasted authority of those divines who represent the Redeemer of the world as little more than a moral reformer, and the Christian faith as a code of ethics differing from the moral system of Moses and the prophets only by an additional motive ; or, rather, by the additional strength and clearness which the historical fact of the Resurrection has given to the same motive." But, as Coleridge points out, the word translated " religion " in our Bible, the Greek word *Threskeia*, really means the outward offices of religion, the ceremonial. For the Jew, St James seems to argue, the outward ceremonial of religion consisted of " the

[4] Mark xii. 29 and 30.

[5] " Pure religion and undefiled before God and the Father is this : To visit the fatherless and widows in their affliction, and to keep himself unspotted from the world."

B

washing of cups, and pots brazen vessels, and tables"; [6] but the inward reality was justice, mercy, and purity of heart. But this, the Apostle evidently thinks, which was the inward reality, the very heart, of the Jews' religion is no more than the outward ceremonial of the Christian's religion. The inward reality there is nothing less than the knowledge and love of God, direct communion with the source of all life. Coleridge remarks very truly that to translate *Threskeia* by our word " religion " here " has the effect of an erroneous translation ; it not only obscures the connection of the passage, and weakens the peculiar force and sublimity of the thought, rendering it comparatively flat and trivial, almost, indeed, tautological, but has occasioned this particular verse to be perverted into a support of a very dangerous error." [7]

Now this error, which Coleridge calls a very dangerous one, the error, namely, of supposing that morality and philanthropy are, by themselves, enough, and that they make up " pure religion," is, in the long run, as dangerous to morality and philanthropy as to religion itself. True religion is the root of all vital morality and all effective philanthropy, and when the root dies the fruit does not endure very long. Our Saviour bids us " seek first the Kingdom of God, and His righteousness, and all these things (the social goods) shall be added unto you." [8] If we reverse the process, and seek first the fruits of social effort, it is not merely that we are in danger of losing God ; we are in danger of losing those social fruits for which we have sacrificed Him Who is our highest good. " What shall it profit a man if he shall gain the whole world, and lose his own soul ? " was Christ's question. Might we not go further and ask what is the state of a man, or of a nation, which, losing God, finds that with Him the world has been lost too ? Now the point I am trying to make is so opposed to the prevailing view to-day, the view entertained by the man in the street, and industriously upheld by the popular Press, that I want to write as plainly as possible. My

[6] Cf. Mark vii. 4.
[7] *Aids to Reflection.* Introductory Aphorisms : Aph. XXIII.
[8] Matt. vi. 33.

readers may not agree with my views. It shall not be my fault if they do not understand what those views are. The popular view, the view championed, as I have said, by the popular Press, is that the orthodox members of the various denominations do little for social betterment, that the Christian religion is not rich in fruits of righteousness, and that people with no religion do as much, and usually more, for their fellow-men than believing Christians. Indeed, a popular writer, whose books sell by hundreds of thousands, said recently, in one of those professions of faith which are so much in favour with our leading novelists to-day, that " it is because the orthodox Christian has given up hope of human nature that he accepts as inevitable in this world just those things which the unorthodox are prepared to fight." But what are those evils in which orthodox Christians acquiesce ? And where can I go to see the unorthodox combating them ? Not, if my experience serves, in Walworth or in Bethnal Green, in Poplar or in Hoxton. Not in the slums of Leeds or Manchester or Liverpool. To speak quite plainly I should say that ninety per cent. and more of the voluntary service of others in England to-day (of other countries I cannot speak from any personal experience) was the work of believing Christians, active members of some congregation, and of orthodox Jews ; of men and women, that is to say, who have a definite belief in God, and whose lives are ruled and directed by that belief. And when that faith dwindles and dies the good works dwindle and die too. Good works seem to me to be the fruits of a faith in God. Let us see if history bears out this view. I follow a line of thought which I owe to Dr. Temple, Archbishop of York.

Of all shameful acts of which human nature is ever guilty, what is the most shameful ? Some would say cannibalism. But that, after all, is the perverted taste of a few very degraded peoples, and they themselves are ashamed of it, and seek to hide it from the eyes of other people. I should say that infanticide was the darkest blot on human nature. And this, be it remembered, has been the crime of highly-civilized nations. There is probably no nobler sentiment in secular literature than Terence's words : " I am a man.

Nothing that concerns man can be of indifference to me."
Yet the poet puts into the mouth of the same character a
direction to his wife that, if the child that will be born
while he is away on a journey should be a boy, it is to be
kept ; if a girl, it is to be destroyed. And among the most
cultured and refined classes in China, after untold centuries
of civilization, infanticide is openly practised. We may be
sure that if Christianity loses its hold on the world, infanticide—either in the form of abortion, or even in the form of
the destruction of superfluous infants—will again be
permitted.

What has most degraded and debased human nature ?
Can we doubt that the bloody sports of the gladiatorial
shows did more than anything else to destroy every noble
feeling ? To take delight daily in the agony and death of
one's fellow-creatures must have brutalized all who took
part. Telemachus, the Christian monk, by his death
cleansed the world of this foul cancer.

What has been the cause of the greatest and most widespread suffering and misery ? Surely what Wesley called
" that monstrous sum of all imaginable villainies," the
slave trade. And awful as were the sufferings of negro
slaves in the Southern States of America, the evils of slavery
under the empires of the old world were infinitely worse.
Now it is a plain historical fact that the abolition of slavery,
so far as it has been abolished, is the fruit of the Evangelical
revival, and of nothing else, and that no other religion, and
no movement of philanthropy apart from religion, has the
least share of the credit.

What has done most to alleviate suffering ? Surely the
hospital movement. And this is wholly and entirely a
product of Christian sentiment. I believe that in quite
modern times the Parsees of India have founded hospitals.
But, while giving them all credit for their humanity, we
cannot deny that the original impulse to relieve the sick
and suffering was wholly Christian. It would be easy to
enumerate many other blessings that the world owes to
Christianity, and to Christianity alone. Such are the winning
for woman her rightful place ; the final condemnation of
those darker forms of vice which disfigured Greek and

Roman civilization and still disgrace China and India ; the recognition of the essential brotherhood of man ; and many others. I do not deny that many so-called Christians are unworthy of the name. But that does not in the least affect my argument. My point is that through the ages fruits of social righteousness have been the fruits of Christianity. It is often said, by secularists, that these have been the fruits rather of civilization than of religion. On the contrary, a very high level of civilization, as under the Roman Empire, or in China, is compatible with an almost complete deadness of the moral consciousness. A casual sentence of Dr. T. R. Glover's, when he is writing of Athens in the age of Pericles, is illuminating. He says : " The horrible condition of the slaves in the silver mines of Attica is sometimes noticed by ancient writers, but there is no indication that it troubled the capitalists or the public conscience."[9] But perhaps the most striking example of the truth which I am seeking to enforce is to be drawn from the religious history of our own country. It would be difficult to exaggerate the spiritual deadness of the nation in the eighteenth century. In the " advertisement " to the first edition of his *Analogy of Religion*, in 1736, just two years before John Wesley's return from Georgia, Dr. Butler wrote : " It is come, I know not how, to be taken for granted, by many persons, that Christianity is not so much a subject for enquiry, but that it is now at length discovered to be fictitious. And, accordingly, they treat it as if, in the present age, this were an agreed point among all people of discernment, and nothing remained but to set it up as a principal subject of mirth and ridicule." And there is abundant evidence of the truth of the statement that " morals were getting out of fashion as much as religion. Society had all the grossness without much of the wit which belonged to the days of the Restoration."[10] And what is true of that small fraction of the nation which in those days passed under the name of "society," was yet

[9] *From Pericles to Philip*, by T. R. Glover. Second Edition, 1918 , p. 44.
[10] *A History of the Four Georges and of William IV*, by Justin McCarthy. Chapter XXX.

more true of the nation at large. Nothing in connection with the eighteenth century strikes one so forcibly as the callousness and brutality, the absence of anything like a social conscience, in connection with prisoners, slaves, paupers, children, those mentally afflicted, and animals. My acquaintance with social and economic history is only an amateur one. But I do not think it would be difficult to prove that, in England, at any rate, the eighteenth century showed not merely no advance in these matters, as compared with pre-Reformation times, but an actual deterioration.   Then came the Evangelical revival, first the Methodist revival, and then the Evangelical revival within the Church of England. Now this revival—for it was one in origin and inspiration if dual in its results— was the work of men more utterly and entirely " other-worldly " than the leaders of any other great movement since the first century. God, the soul, sin that separates from God, redemption, these were their pre-occupations. No men ever had their eyes more averted from this world, or more set on Heaven, than the Evangelical clergy.   And what were their social fruits ?   They emancipated the slave, and cleansed the prisons, and humanized our blood-stained criminal law, and re-founded a system of national education, and initiated factory legislation. However much these reforms may have drawn to themselves the support of social reformers unmoved by religious motives—and what always surprises me, and what will, I think, surprise all disinterested students who pay careful attention to the point, is the small number of merely *secular* reformers as opposed to religious workers in the early stages of all these reforms—the plain and indubitable fact remains that they had their origin in an intense personal religion, an intense love of God and desire for His glory, and would either never have been begun at all, or at any rate would have been long delayed, but for the religious movement.

And what has been true in the past is true to-day. The idea that members of the various religious denominations— churchgoers, in fact, in the widest sense of the word " church" —are selfishly concerned with their own salvation, and that, judged by the test of good works and active philanthropy, people who attend no place of worship are just as good, and probably better, than those who profess and practise a definite religion, is a pure delusion unsupported by any vestige of evidence. Here and there a man or woman, brought up in an intensely Christian atmosphere, or in an atmosphere of orthodox Judaism, and having lost religious faith in later years, will continue the habits of generous giving and of active service learned in youth. But these are exceptions. They always remind me of trees uprooted by winter storms which bud and bear leaves while lying on the ground, because they are still full of sap. *They do not put out leaves or blossom a second year.* So the second generation, in such cases, seldom retain those habits of philanthropy (love of man) which seem to me to be very definitely the fruit of religion (love of God). The point is one which each reader should consider for himself and bring to the test of daily experience. But it may be worth while to quote three pieces of evidence, the first two of which are some eight years old, while the last came to hand only a few days ago. Billed to speak, in 1922, in a certain town far distant from Manchester, on social questions, I got a letter, a few days before the meeting, asking me to appeal for workers for the " Play Centres " for poor children, for " it is little to the credit of the churches that we should be so short of helpers." I wrote asking for an interview, and then asked the lady responsible for the letter why she looked to the churches for workers for a type of work which most of the churches were already doing week by week the year round. Surely, I said, it would be more reasonable for her to seek support, for her non-sectarian work, from people not connected with any place of worship. She replied, with great scorn, that I could not know much of life if I expected any help from that quarter. I did not expect it. But I did not tell her so.

Not long after, speaking in quite another part of England, I was asked to appeal for workers for the *Civic League of Help*. The writer said : "You would think that this kind of work, being wholly unsectarian and non-political, would appeal to those who cannot accept the dogmas of the

churches. But we have to depend altogether on the
churches for our workers."

These two pieces of evidence are seven years old. Let
me come to the present time. A few days ago a man whom
I just know by sight called on me. He is the head of a big
business in another city, and has branches of his business
in Manchester, and in at least one other place. He apolo-
gized for calling, but said he had recently seen, in a news-
paper, a statement to the effect that I had claimed ninety
per cent. of philanthropic work in England for the members
of various Christian denominations. Was it true, he asked,
that I had made such a claim. I replied that it was perfectly
true. He went on to say that when he first read the paragraph he was greatly startled, and regretted that a clergyman should have made it. But the more he thought of the
matter the more he was forced to admit the claim to be
true. " I am nearer seventy than sixty," he said, " and
when I ask myself the plain question : ' When and where
have I seen self-sacrificing work done for other people by
those without religious faith,' I am bound to reply that I
have never seen it at any time nor in any place. In the
town where I live, and here in Manchester, when I was a
boy, and now that I am old, it is and always has been
true, now I really face the question, that unselfish giving,
whether of money or of service, is a fruit of religion."

I have no experience of foreign countries. But some years
ago a man, well qualified to speak, said exactly the same
about France. He declared that French Protestants con-
tributed, both in money and in effort, beyond all proportion
to their numerical strength, but that, apart from that,
ninety-five per cent. of the charitable work of France was
the work of the practising Catholic, and that to extract a
franc from the ordinary man or woman divorced from
religion was as hard as to draw blood from a stone.

If the argument of this chapter is correct, we may conclude
that neither morality nor philanthropy, nor both together,
can be regarded as religion, nor as a substitute for it. And,
further, we may claim that these things themselves are
fruits of religion and tend to wither and disappear when
their true root, a disinterested love for God, is lacking.

May not one of the reasons for the weakness of the various branches of the Christian Church to-day be this, that bishops and clergy have often been so anxious to " apply Christianity to every department of life " that they have been more active in serving tables than in " giving them-selves continually to prayer, and to the ministry of the word."[11] I do not deny that Christianity can be and should be applied to every sphere of life.   Quite the contrary ; " I am not ashamed of the gospel of Christ, for it is the power of God unto salvation."[12] I believe, that is to say, that a true, deep, and sincere personal religion is the only cure for all our ills.   But, if I may be allowed to state so obvious a truism, the religion must exist before it can be applied. And so it is of supreme importance that those whose business lies in the production of personal religion should not allow themselves to be drawn away from their great tasks of conversion and edification to other work.   If the reader will carefully examine all arguments which he hears in favour of clergy and ministers of religion taking an active part in politics and social questions, he will, I think, find that they owe what force they seem to possess to a deep-seated confusion as to the nature of " the Church."   " The Church," we are told, must touch life at every point. " The Church " has a message for all classes.   All good work is, we are assured, " Church work " in the truest sense. This is true.   But it is also true that the Church is the body of Christ ; and " the body is one, and hath many mem-bers " ;[13] and again :   " all members have not the same office."[14] The fact that work is good work, and needs to be done, is no sort of argument in favour of its being done by the clergy to the neglect of their own vitally important work of preaching, teaching, pastoral visitation, and ministering the sacraments.   There is no more reason why the Church should use one class of her limbs (members) with which to do all classes of work than why a man should try to stand on his head, or use his feet to play the piano with.   Yet this deep-seated confusion between the Church and clergy meets us at every turn.   Soon after the General

---

[11] Acts vi. 4.   [12] Rom. i. 16.
[13] I Cor. xii. 12.   [14] Rom. xii. 4.

Strike, a visiting bishop, speaking at a Diocesan Conference, began his speech with the words : " I am here to protest against the warning off of the Church from the area of political and social effort. And when I speak of the Church I mean the laity as well as the clergy, Nonconformists as well as Anglicans." But who has ever suggested that the entire nation, clergy and laity, Anglicans and Nonconformists, should be warned off politics and social subjects ? Clearly the speaker used the word Church the first time as meaning bishops and clergy, and in the second half of his sentence as meaning all who profess and call themselves Christians. If this confusion were merely a verbal one it would not matter. But it has two fatal results. Firstly, it encourages many of the laity—not all, thank God, nor nearly all, but certainly many—to leave all good works to the clergy, and themselves to devote all time and effort to getting and spending, to the lasting impoverishment of their lives. And, secondly, it encourages the clergy in neglecting their own work of dealing with individual souls, to do all kinds of work which ought to be left to deeply converted laymen. A brother clergyman, who heard me talking in this strain, once said to me with some irritation : " It's all very well talking like that, but where are the laity willing to do the work ? " But surely if there are not enough deeply converted laymen and laywomen to do their proper work, that is in itself a proof that we clergy have not done our special work. We seem to be involved in a vicious circle. There are not enough converted men to do the world's work. So we clergy leave our special task of conversion and try to do the layman's work for him. And so the number of the converted laity is still further decreased. And so the clergy are yet more drawn away to do social work. When shall we clergy have faith to break by force out of this vicious circle and to cry : " God forbid that I should glory (*i.e.* that I should rely on, or have confidence in, anything), save in the cross of our Lord Jesus Christ, by whom the world is crucified unto me, and I unto the world " ? [15]

I said, at the beginning of this chapter, that I feared

[15] Gal. vi. 14.

I might have puzzled and alienated some of my readers by my criticisms of a " here-and-now " religion. I have no fear of offending or puzzling any of my readers, at least among the laity, by what I have just said. I believe that the vast majority of the religious laity desire that the clergy should confine themselves to their definitely spiritual work. I may perhaps be allowed to quote something that I wrote nearly twenty years ago. It runs : " The layman who is not a faddist has, I suspect, a secret impatience of the parson who is active in everything but his own business. He looks with wonder on a man who has so much time for what does not concern him and so little for what does. He marvels that a parson should turn from work so interesting, so much needed, and so thankfully welcomed, to do work which others could do as well or better." If I am right in believing this to be the attitude of most thoughtful laymen, then the laity are surely right. For the great need of the world is for God. The Scotch Shorter Catechism declares that man's purpose and end is "To glorify God, and to enjoy Him for ever." But if this is true, then nothing can go well with society, nor with the individual, where God is forgotten. No matter how little the message may commend itself to modern ears, and no matter how utterly it may run counter to the popular catchwords of the moment, I am sure that it is true that other-worldliness is the truest worldly wisdom, and to love God with all one's heart, and with all one's soul, and with all one's mind, is the one sure and certain path to lead a man to love his neighbour as himself. Philanthropy is not religion, but religion, disinterested love of God for His own sake, will very surely prove to be the best philanthropy.

CHAPTER III

CAN GOD BE KNOWN?

WE have defined religion as a disinterested delight in God for His own sake. And we have examined the claim of morality and philanthropy to be true religion, and have rejected that claim on the ground that they are rather to be regarded as fruits of religion which tend to disappear when God, the true goal of religion, is forgotten. It would be well if we could now go straight to that goal, and discuss how God may be known, and what are the fruits of that knowledge. But there is still a preliminary enquiry which is necessary. For religion to-day is weakened not merely by the prevailing worldliness, and by the rush and racket of our times, but by a deep-seated agnosticism which still survives as an evil legacy from the nineteenth century. Many people are hindered in their search for God by a lingering doubt whether there is a God, or at any rate whether God can be known by man. And this is the question which we must face squarely before we can tackle any other aspect of our subject.

Now, of course, it was one of the axioms of late nineteenth-century materialism that even if God exists He cannot be known. For all knowledge, they argued, comes to us through the senses, and anything that can be an object of knowledge must be capable of being seen, heard, tasted, smelt, or touched. But since God, even if He exists, is not an object of sense perception, He cannot be known. And Huxley coined the word " agnostic," *i.e. one who does not and cannot know,* to express the only truly scientific attitude towards all spiritual realities. It is impossible to exaggerate the arrogance of tone with which many men of science, during the last quarter of last century, attacked every form of revealed religion. Huxley especially allowed, to those who differed from him, only three alternatives ; they were either too lazy to study the evidence, or too stupid to understand it, or too dishonest to admit that they were wrong. And Tyndall, even if he spoke and wrote on religious and theological subjects less than Huxley, adopted an even more truculent tone when he did handle them. And Herbert Spencer, W. K. Clifford, and other leading men of the time were all in the same story. But to-day the entire philosophy of nineteenth-century materialism is dead, utterly discredited and rejected by all competent critics. That being so, it might seem unnecessary even to refer to them now. Unfortunately, that is not so. There are, to-day, men and women in every walk of life who learned all that they know of science and philosophy between 1880 and 1900, and others who were taught by those whose views were formed during that period. Many such men and women have done excellent work in their own lines as journalists, in business, in the professions, or as teachers of some specialized department of knowledge. But the pressure of their daily life and their daily work has prevented them from keeping abreast of the general movements of theology, philosophy, and science. So they go on repeating the doctrines of nineteenth-century materialism as if they were the last word in human knowledge, blandly unconscious of the fact that they are quite hopelessly out of date. It would not be difficult to quote instances, collected during the last twelve months, of leading men in every department of life, in politics, literature, science, and art, laying down the law on theology, and its relations with science and philosophy, with as complete an ignorance of the best modern thought on the subject as would distinguish a man who lectured on naval matters with no more knowledge than he could gather from confused memories of Marryat's novels. But, unfortunately, the ordinary man who reads an attack on religion, in his evening paper, and sees that it has been written by a noted surgeon, or by a novelist who has produced a number of best-sellers, never pauses to ask whether there is any reason for supposing that the man has either read widely or thought seriously on the subject since he left college forty years ago.

But, to come more close to our subject, what can be said

in answer to the claims of the nineteenth-century agnostic
that God is necessarily unknowable ? Firstly, we can boldly
assert that the statement is itself profoundly unscientific.
It is no part of the duty of science to declare *a priori* what
can and what cannot be known. The man of science should
enquire what, as a matter of fact, men and women claim to
know, and should investigate those claims to see if they are
or are not well founded. When the materialists of last
century denied human immortality, moral freedom, and the
possibility of prayer being efficacious, they did so not in
loyalty to observed facts, but in the interests of their own
theories. Much, even in the realms of natural science, which
the school of Huxley scornfully denied, and refused even to
investigate, is now accepted and believed by all competent
observers.

Secondly, we may say that even in the hey-day of the
" oppositions of science falsely so called," the men who
really ranked as philosophical thinkers, and not merely as
experts in some branch of natural science trying their hands
at philosophy in their spare time, rejected the entire scheme
of a mechanistic universe. Such men as T. H. Green,
Edward Caird, Earl Balfour (then Mr. A. J. Balfour), James
Ward, and many others regarded the philosophy of the
Huxley-Tyndall school with contempt. And rightly so.
The discoveries of men of science during the last half of the
nineteenth century were wonderful, and the practical fruits
of those discoveries, which we enjoy in everyday life, rightly
rouse our admiration and claim our gratitude. But *the facts
of science* are one thing ; *the systems of philosophy* which men
erect on a basis of these facts are something very different.
And it must be admitted that the philosophy which men of
science championed some fifty years ago was crude and
childish in the extreme. Professor J. Arthur Thomson says
truly, in his Gifford Lectures for 1915–16, that " some of the
ablest scientific minds the world has known have betrayed
in their would-be philosophical deliverances an extraordinary naïveté." [1]

Thirdly, we cannot merely say that the attitude of the

[1] *The System of Animate Nature.* Williams & Norgate, 1920.
Vol. I., p. 38.

men we are criticizing was itself essentially unscientific ; we cannot merely record that the best philosophical thinking of the times was against it ; we can go further and see where the mistake, which these men made, lay, and what it was. They thought that their scientific theories gave an actual picture of the real world. But a scientific theory is much more like a *map* than a *picture*. It is a convenient method of grasping certain aspects of reality with which we happen to be concerned. *But the value of a map may largely depend on the number of things it can ignore without affecting the accuracy of those details it includes.* Any airman would prefer a modern map to one of the picturesque old maps of the seventeenth century which showed elephants and lions in the forests, and dolphins and whales gambolling and blowing round the coasts. But surely it would be absurd to deny that there were tigers in India because none are shown on the best ordinance survey maps issued to-day. All our theories, historical, scientific, economic, æsthetic, ethical, or religious, are merely efforts to hold and describe varying aspects of one full, rich, varied reality which still eludes our efforts to include it whole and complete in a single picture. Nor would it be true to say that we are always trying to include in our picture more and more aspects of reality. Progress is often made by ignoring all but a very few of those aspects.[2] But it is mere folly to deny the existence of all aspects of reality which do not happen to fall within our particular province. Yet this is just what the men of the later part of the nineteenth century did, and Professor Whitehead says of that period : " Clear-sighted men, of the sort who are so clearly wrong, now proclaimed that the secrets of the physical universe were finally disclosed. If only you ignored everything which refused to come into line your powers of explanation were unlimited."[3]

Fourthly, we may say—and this is a thing I would lay special stress on—that in the conflict of science and religion

---

[2] Appallingly difficult as are the mathematics of relativity, the whole relativity theory is a drastic simplification of natural science, and consists of treating all problems of physics as purely geometrical problems, the metric relations of a continuous manifold.

[3] *Science and the Modern World.* Cambridge, 1925, p. 126.

in the last quarter of last century, on such topics as God, the soul, moral freedom, and the possibility of prayer producing any effect, the assumption that the men of science were always right and the theologians always wrong is not far from being the exact opposite of the truth. Whatever views a man may hold on these topics, he would no more dream of trying to defend them to-day with arguments based on the materialistic philosophy of the nineteenth century, the philosophy which, in Huxley's words, made for the " banishment from all regions of human thought of what we call spirit and spontaneity," than he would think of quoting in defence of his views mediæval doctrines of witchcraft. That philosophy is utterly discredited to-day. And it is discredited for the very reasons for which theologians rejected it when it was at its hey-day of renown,[4] namely, because along with the things which it claimed to have got rid of—God, immortality, and moral freedom— it also, if accepted, destroyed all distinctions of right and wrong, and left no room even for rationality.[5]

This discussion of nineteenth-century attacks on religion might seem out of date, a mere slaying of the already twice slain. But that is not so. Many present-day criticisms of revealed religion are equally unphilosophical and in- consistent. There are many men writing to-day who first enunciate theories, metaphysical or psychological, which

[4] Dr Inge says, of this period, with absolute truth, that " the naturalists of Queen Victoria's reign built on their scientific studies a superstructure of badly designed philosophy, an incongruous mixture of atomism and pantheism, which the religious mind rightly refused to accept."—*The Church and the World*. Longmans, 1927, p. 244.

[5] Huxley himself seems to have come in the end to recognize this, for in his Romanes Lecture in 1894 he made the surprising discovery that " the ethical progress of society depends, not on imitating the cosmic process, still less in running away from it, but in combating it." How man, who was supposed to be no more than a cog in that one great machine which we call the universe, could combat the cosmic process, or how, in a universe utterly devoid of spirit or spontaneity, any one part could be supposed to combat the rest, or what exactly we are to understand by " running away from the cosmic process," we need not pause to enquire. Dr. D'Arcy is surely right when he says, in his *Short Study of Ethics*, that "such a conclusion as this reduces the whole doctrine to an absurdity."

implicitly deny God, moral freedom, immortality, rationality, and all æsthetic values. And then, having emptied life of all that makes it worth living, they proceed to bring back so much of what they have denied as they themselves value by vague talk about " idealism," " mysticism," or some similar expression. They do not seem to recognize that the same appeal, no matter to what it is made, which lets in goodness, truth, duty, and the æsthetic values, things which they value, lets in at the same time God, immortality, and moral freedom ; things which they deny and reject.[6]

So, when I am assured that " science has proved " this or that to be untrue, I always put the following questions to my critic :

(1) How has science *proved* this ? Is the appeal to well-established facts of science, or merely to a theory which some man of science has erected on the basis of those facts ; and which other men of science, quite as capable, reject ?

(2) Is my critic prepared to accept to the full the conclusions which spring from his own theory ? Or does he claim, at one and the same time, to apply his theory when it seems to destroy Christianity, but to suspend or ignore it when it renders his own beliefs absurd ?

(3) Is it not a fact that the whole trend of philosophy, and of the best scientific thought of to-day, is towards a spiritual interpretation of reality ?

For one thing is absolutely certain, namely, that science has not proved either that there is no God or that He cannot be known.

" But," it will be asked, " how is this statement affected by the new attacks on religion from the side of psychology ? Hitherto you have only considered the out-of-date materialism of the nineteenth century. But is it not a fact that

---

[6] It would be utterly impossible to name all the examples of this noble, but irrational, holding-on to the highest things in spite of an intellectual faith which leaves no room for them. But three glaring examples may be quoted, namely, the Hon. Bertrand Russell's much admired but utterly irrational essay, " The Free Man's Worship " (*Philosophical Essays*. Longmans, 1910), *Modern Science and Materialism*, by Hugh Elliot, about the last attempt to defend materialism (Longmans, 1919), and *Vicisti, Galilæe?*, by E. B. Powley (Kegan Paul, 1929.)

modern psychology has proved that the idea of God is merely a projection of the father-complex, and all reasoning in defence of Christianity merely an *a posteriori* attempt to justify by argument opinions dictated to us by irrational likes and dislikes which lie hidden in our subconsciousness."

It is impossible to discuss all these questions in detail. Nor would it be desirable to do so. If I could answer all objections that have ever been raised against religion, from the dawn of history to this moment, the reader might be confronted by something fresh to-morrow. And however convincing my refutation might be, my reader would probably be left with an uneasy feeling that they had only heard one side, and that the arguments against a belief in God might be more convincing in the mouth of someone who believed in them. It is much better that each one of us should face these problems for himself. But the following suggestions may help those who are confronted with attacks on religion from the psychological side.

(1) *Many psychologists fall into what may be called the " fallacy of abstraction."* By that I mean that just as the physicists and biologists of last century began by abstracting, from the whole of reality, some limited number of physical or biological factors, and then, at the end of the discussion, denied that any other factors existed in the real universe, so many psychologists, rightly holding that psychology is concerned only with " states of mind," and that the existence or non-existence of an " ego," or of a real world, are not psychological problems at all, make the mistake, at the end of the discussion, of declaring that God, the soul, etc. are merely the illegitimate projections of states of mind. Psychologists, like other men of science, do not always remember that their science gives us a *map*, not a *portrait*, of reality.

(2) *All theories based on the irrationality of mental processes destroy themselves.* Huxley denied, in his theory of thought as an epiphenomenon, that the mind played any effective part in the world. A man's mental process might be compared to the looking-glass over his mantelpiece. It *reflects* all that goes on but does not itself *cause* any movement. But by demonstrating the supposed impotence of

mind he demonstrated the absurdity of his own conclusions. Many psychologists fall into the same error. A brilliant young psychologist spent some time demonstrating to me the necessarily irrational nature of all my beliefs. He said he was sure I was honest in my faith but my beliefs were merely the result of purely irrational desires and repulsions in the subconscious. When he finished I asked him if the same was true of his psychological theories ; were they also irrational outcrops from the subconscious ; and, if not, why not ? He had, of course, no answer. He had already successfully destroyed the basis of all rational discussion.

(3) *Psychology is a very young science, and along with much that is valuable present-day psychology contains a high proportion of rubbish.* Anyone who reads, at once widely and thoughtfully, in modern psychology, must be struck by the large proportion of statements made by some of even the most famous writers for which there is no sort of proof or evidence. Explanations are offered, as if they were necessary truths, of which one can only say : " Well, that may be true, but there is no kind of proof of it, and the exact opposite would sound equally convincing." Psychologists, like other men of science, sometimes mistake ingenious hypotheses for convincing proofs.

(4) *The established facts of psychology are one thing ; its various hypotheses are another thing altogether ; and the metaphysical system which may be erected on the basis of those facts and those hypotheses is yet a third thing, and distinct altogether from either of them.* Here it may be worth while recalling the remarks of Dr. Inge quoted on p. 32. For however valuable many of the practical fruits of psychology may be, some of its practitioners to-day are building " a superstructure of badly-designed philosophy, an incongruous mixture of atomism and pantheism," and the religious mind will now, as in the last century, do well to refuse to accept it.

So I would urge my readers to be on their guard against " oppositions of science falsely so called." [7] No sane Christian wishes to shut his eyes to the triumphs of knowledge gained by natural science. On the contrary, all truth

[7] I Tim. vi. 20.

must be God's truth, and the Church should welcome every
addition to human knowledge, and build it into the fabric
of her faith. Dr. Temple says : " In the flower of the
Middle Ages philosophers had achieved a systematic unity
of existing knowledge, under the reign of Theology, the
Queen of the Sciences, such as has never been repeated."[8]
And I believe that we are on the threshold of a great era of
constructive theological thinking, comparable to the Alex-
andrine period of the second and third centuries, or the
Scholastic period referred to by Dr. Temple ; yet greater
than either, as our task of achieving a correlation of science,
history, ethics, philosophy, æsthetics, and religion is greater
than theirs. And I believe that the first steps towards such
a unification of knowledge are much nearer than most
people think, though the attainment of the goal is far off.
But nothing but harm is done by hasty and one-sided
attempts at a synthesis which leaves out man's highest
and best knowledge. For myself I can only say that after
thirty years, during which the literature of the so-called
conflict of religion and science has been my chief study,
I do not believe that there is a word in modern science
which need hinder any man from accepting the full Christian
faith.

Perhaps some of my readers, especially those whose faith
has been shaken, but who do earnestly desire to believe,
will think that I go too far in saying this. " Surely," they
will exclaim, " it is an established fact that modern views
about the evolution of man, and modern discoveries as to
the distance of the stars, and the existence of other stellar
universes as large as our own, have shaken the Christian
faith to its foundations." I can only reply that it is *a very
commonly asserted opinion* that such is the case ; it is most
certainly not *an established fact*. Thus, Dr. Inge writes,
" it was a shock to many to hear that the human race
had developed out of non-human ancestors ; but the
question is only about the methods of creation ; Darwinism
has inflicted no injury on the Christian faith." [9] And Dr.
Temple, discussing the statement that modern knowledge

[8] *Christianity and the State*. Macmillan, 1928, p. 13.
[9] *The Church and the World*. Longmans, 1927, p. 157.

as to the size of the universe has rendered faith in the Christian revelation impossible, says : " I cannot believe that the Christians of the twentieth century are going to have any special difficulties with astronomy."[10]

I have no desire to encourage an easily held and uncritical faith. Quite the contrary. I am convinced that there is nothing more vital in religion than entire mental honesty. But much of the vague agnosticism, and religious unsettlement, which is so common to-day might much more reasonably be described as " easily held and uncritical" than the faith of any Christian I have ever met.

But when once we have cleared our minds of the vague agnosticism which still persists as an evil legacy from the nineteenth century, we are in a position to recognize some most striking and heartening facts. And first and foremost we have the unqestionable fact that, down the entire course of history, man stands revealed as pre-eminently *a religious or God-serving being*. This is true of man everywhere and at all times. Even the lowly-developed, ape-like Neanderthal or Mousterian men—those men of a quarter of a million years ago, whom Sir Arthur Conan Doyle has made familiar to everyone by his book, *The Lost World*, and by the film based on that book—have left evidence behind them that they entertained beliefs about the immortality of the soul, and about a life after death, and so, probably, about a god or gods also. And as soon as man emerges into the light of history, and as far back as we can pierce the gloom of prehistory, man's noblest buildings have been his temples, and his highest achievements in all the arts have been produced under the stimulus of religious emotion. If I am told that religion has also been the cause of man's worst excesses, that no wars have been so cruel and so bloodstained as wars of religion, and that there is no crime of which man is capable which has not been committed in the name of religion, I shall not deny it. Rather I shall claim the fact as evidence of just the point I am trying to make.

[10] Article on " The Faith of the Twentieth Century," in the volume *The Future of the Church of England*, edited by Sir James Marchant. Longmans, 1926, p. 35.

Men do not wage great wars, nor commit atrocious crimes, for things in which they have no belief. As Mr. G. K. Chesterton has wisely pointed out, the three things for which man has been prepared to go to the greatest lengths, whether of heroism or of baseness, have been his child, his wife, and his God. Unless we are to declare that love of wife and love of child are necessarily delusions, we must not say that the existence of crimes due to religion proves belief in God to be either irrational or evil. I am not, of course, claiming that because men have been prepared to endure and to inflict terrible sufferings under the influence of religious beliefs that therefore those beliefs are true. I am merely rebutting the argument, often used by atheist lecturers, that because of such crimes religious beliefs *must be false*. The fact that man is essentially a god-seeking and god-serving being is a very striking fact of human nature which no one who desires a really scientific view of life, a view, that is to say, that takes account of all the facts, can afford to ignore. Nor is its weight and importance in any way lessened by the way in which the populations of many large towns in Europe and America seem to be losing the sense of God's presence. Mr. Kipling is always worth attending to, not merely as an interesting writer of fiction, but as a very shrewd student of human nature. He says, in one of his stories, " The Conversion of Aurelian McGoggin ": " In Town where there is nothing but machinery and asphalt and building—all shut in by fog—naturally a man grows to think that there is no one higher than himself, and that the Metropolitan Board of Works made everything. But in India, where you really see humanity—raw, brown, naked humanity—with nothing between it and the blazing sky, and only the used-up, over-handled earth underfoot, the notion somehow dies out, and most folk come back to simpler theories." [11] This, in spite of the intentionally light and flippant form of expression, is a profound truth. The life of the masses in our big towns is an essentially unnatural one. There are other powers besides the power to know God which may become blunted by the shallow, restricted, unnatural life of wage-

[11] *Plain Tales from the Hills.*

earners in big cities. If we want to know what man's natural powers are we must study man under not too unnatural conditions.

A second fact, not less striking than the universality of belief in a god or gods, is the fact that in all ages and in all nations many of the noblest men and women have found in their faith in God at once the most precious thing in life and the inspiration of all their activity. Can they all have been deluded? Can a delusion have borne such fruit? "Do men gather grapes of thorns or figs of thistles?"[12]

But there is yet a third fact, which is, to my mind, the most striking of all. It is impossible to have even a slight acquaintance with non-Christian religious literature without recognizing the identity of religious experience under all differences, and even contradictions, of credal belief. Whether a man is a Christian, a Jew, a Mohammedan, a Buddhist, a Hindu, or a follower of one of the religions which we call by the general name of "heathen religions," his religious experience, as distinct from mere religious belief or opinion, is curiously identical everywhere. This assertion, which would have shocked our grandparents, may perhaps surprise some even of modern readers. One here and there may be found to object: "But Buddhists, Hindus, and heathen idolaters worship false gods!" I shall reply that there is no such thing as a false god. There are false ideas about God. But there is but one God, and, everywhere and always, when and where man has first-hand experience of God, it is of that one true God of whom he has experience, just as when and where a man sees the sun, and rejoices in its light and warmth, it is one and the same sun that he sees which all men see, no matter by what name they call him nor what their astronomical theories. It is impossible to illustrate this truth here and now. To produce a few examples from the Old Testament, from Mohammedan, Buddhist, and Hindu sacred books, and from purely heathen literature, would look like special pleading. To quote adequately would be to reproduce the devotional literature of all time. But one piece of evidence is worth citing.

[12] Matt. vii. 16.

Such a writer as Miss Evelyn Underhill,[13] when writing of mystical experience—of direct experience, that is to say, of God—can quote Pagan and Christian, Hindu and Buddhist, orthodox Mohammedan and freethinking Sufi, ancient Jewish prophet, and modern American mystic, and find in all the same witness to a God " in Whom we live and move and have our being." Professor Eddington says, with absolute truth, that " there are some to whom the sense of a Divine presence, irradiating the soul, is one of the most obvious things of experience."[14] And though the power thus to experience the presence of God varies, like all other human powers, in different individuals, yet I believe that it is not wholly lacking in any man. A former colleague of mine once beautifully expressed this truth when he said in a sermon : " There is nothing so native to man as God, nor anywhere where he is so completely at home." Some nations possess the power to a greater degree than others. When we speak of the Jews as God's chosen people, we are only expressing, in other words, the fact that they, as a nation, had a genius for religion. Not for theology, which is the science of religion, but for religious experience, firsthand knowledge of God. And as among nations, so among individuals ; there are religious geniuses. But I would reassert my belief that none are without some power to know God, though many have allowed the power to become atrophied. " For they shall all know me, from the least of them unto the greatest of them, saith the Lord."[15]

I would therefore urge my readers to shake off fear, and doubt, and hesitation, and to launch out boldly upon the ocean which is God. So doing they will, like Columbus, find a new world beyond all that they hoped or looked for. I believe a deep-seated agnosticism, a vital scepticism which finds not even one thing needful, is the distinctive disease of our times.[16] It is partly an evil legacy of the

[13] See *Mysticism*. Methuen, 1911. *The Mystic Way*. Dent & Sons, 1913. *The Life of the Spirit and the Life of To-day*. Methuen, 1922.
[14] *The Nature of the Physical World*. Cambridge University Press, 1928, p. 322.
[15] Jeremiah xxxi. 34.
[16] *Cf.* the character of Norris Carthew, sketched at the opening of Chapter XXII in R. L. Stevenson's book, *The Wrecker*.

nineteenth century. It may be—I think it is—partly a
nervous disease due to the fact that souls made to be
satisfied by God alone are being fed with mere distractions,
pleasures, things which cannot nourish nor sustain life.
Agnosticism of the type common to-day—not the active,
robust disbelief of the last quarter of last century, but the
spirit that says : " Well, I don't know ! One doesn't know
what to think ! "—is a kind of mental debility due to mal-
nutrition. The whole world to-day needs a great dose of
God. " But without faith it is impossible to please Him ;
for he that cometh to God must first believe that He is,
and that He is a rewarder of them that diligently seek
Him."[17]

[17] Heb. xi. 6.

CHAPTER IV

GOD AND MAN

IF the knowledge and love of God is man's best good, the sum of all other goods, indeed man's very life, life eternal enjoyed here and now, what can we say about that knowledge ?   What are its elements ?   How does it come and how may it be enjoyed ?

Perhaps a story will make a good introduction to what I want to say at this point.   When I first went to a public school, a small boy and low in the school, there was, in the sixth form, a boy distinguished neither in games nor in work !   I don't mean that he was specially bad at either. He was neither at the bottom of the form nor at the top ; he played games, but not well enough to get his colours. He was just an average, middle-class public-school boy. Yet in one thing he was far from the average.   All the school knew him to be religious.   I do not think he obtruded it at all.   Yet of its entire sincerity and genuineness no one had any doubt.   At that time I had, of course, no real personal religion, though I had plenty of religious habits. But I was interested, even then, in the matter, and one day when I managed to get the prefect by himself I asked him what exactly " being religious " meant.   He was a pleasant fellow, not too proud to talk to small boys low in the school, and he gave me the sort of answer that anyone would expect.   He said that if a boy wanted to be religious there were some things he must not do ; he must not cheat at work, or tell lies, or swear, or listen to dirty talk.   I knew all that and it seemed very uninteresting ; and so I asked if that were all.   Then suddenly his face changed and he said : " No, it is not.   Do you really want to know what religion is ?   Well, it's waking up in the middle of the night and remembering that you

42

belong to God, and turning over and going to sleep happy
because of it."

I believe I give his very words. Yet though they impressed
themselves on my mind, I did not think much of them at
the time. And many people to whom I have since quoted
them have described them as sentimental. Yet the longer
I live the more I come to believe that they represent the
most fundamental relationship between man and God.
" I am my Lord's, and He is mine," is, and I believe always
has been, the cry of the religious man. Professor W. R.
Matthews speaks of " the feeling of dependence in which
many, following Schleiermacher, would find the germ of
religion."[1] He is surely right. And yet the word dependence alone is hardly adequate. It needs the addition of
some such word as happy or joyful. It is a mutual relationship between the soul and God, and an altogether joyful one.
This joyful sense of dependence upon God inspires the
prophet when he says : " One shall say I am the Lord's ;
and another shall call himself by the name of Jacob ;
and another shall subscribe with his hand unto the Lord,
and surname himself by the name of Israel."[2] It inspires
St. Paul's repeated descriptions of himself as God's bondman. We hear its echo in the Blessed Virgin's words :
" Behold the handmaid of the Lord."[3] And in our own day
no mission hymn expresses the first raptures of the converted man more fully than one which says :

"I am Thine, O Lord, I have heard Thy voice,"

or at least expresses that thought in some similar words.
Indeed, it seems really as if this joyful sense of dependence
on God, of being owned by God, of being the bondman of
Him " Whose service is perfect freedom," were the fundamental emotion in all religion. And it hardly needs pointing
out that this emotion is not peculiar to Judaism and
Christianity. Wherever man has worshipped a god or gods
he has delighted to " subscribe with his hand " to his god, and
surname himself with the names of his chosen deity. This

---

[1] *Studies in Christian Philosophy*. Macmillan, 1921, p. 25.
[2] Isaiah xliv. 5. [3] Luke i. 38.

emotion, like all emotions, is capable of displaying itself on very varying levels. Among very primitive savages delight in a man's tribal deity, and the sense of belonging to that deity, may show itself in nothing more exalted than the conviction that, if it comes to a fight, " my Ju-ju will beat your Ju-ju." And even in the Old Testament the sense of belonging to Jehovah, and enjoying His protection and favour, shows itself at times in unlovely forms. But we do not judge, nor condemn, man's other emotions and beliefs because they show themselves, in children, in childish forms. Why should we have a different standard for man's religious emotions and beliefs ? And as with individuals, so with nations : " When I was a child, I spake as a child, I understood as a child, I thought as a child ; but when I became a man, I put away childish things."[4] We need not be surprised that this particular piece of religious experience, namely, the joyful sense of dependence upon God, often shows itself, in the Old Testament, in childish and crude forms. Rather we should be surprised if it did not. For, indeed, the criticism of the Old Testament, and of the conceptions of God found in the Old Testament, which lay stress on the low moral ideals of the early Hebrews, and which describe Jehovah as " a bloodthirsty tribal deity, delighting in the slaughter of his foes," simply prove two things. Firstly, they prove that the critics who talk in this way have never really learned the lesson Charles Darwin taught, namely, the lesson of evolution from lower to higher forms, since to expect the morality of A.D. 1900 from the people of 1000 B.C. is as unreasonable as to look for a man among the giant reptiles of the Jurassic age. And, secondly, it proves that these critics know nothing of the religious literature of nations contemporary with the Jewish prophets and psalmists of the Old Testament. For the marvel of the Jewish scriptures is not that here and there they show traces of the age in which they were written, but that even at their lowest—and how much more at their highest—they stand so immeasurably above the religious literature of any and of all other nations of pre-Christian times. Where else, outside the Old Testament, shall we find anything to

[4] 1 Cor. xiii. 11.

compare with Genesis xxxii. (Jacob at Mahanaim and at Peniel) ; Exodus xxxiii., 12 to end (Moses' vision of God) ; Isaiah vi. and Isaiah xii.; Psalms li., ciii. and cxxxix. ; and a hundred other passages of the Old Testament. It does not matter, to my argument, in the very least who wrote them, nor whether any given passage has any, or if so what, basis in actual history. What stands out clearly is that here we have first-hand experience of God, the very stuff of which religion is made. The Greek is not more indisputably the teacher of art to the world than the Jew is the teacher of religion. Yet, as we have said, wherever and whenever man is studied he is found to be pre-eminently a God-seeking, God-serving being. And the most elementary, the most fundamental form of religious experience, seems to be a sense of being God's man, God's bond-servant, owned by God, and safe in His keeping.

There is, however, another form of religious experience, no less universal, and nearly though not quite as fundamental as the sense of being God-owned. I mean the sense of sin. Now what is it that distinguishes the sense of sin from many closely-allied emotions ; from remorse, and shame, and despair, and regret at the results of our actions ? Is it not just that element in our emotions which the psalmist expresses when he cries :

" Against Thee only have I sinned and done this evil in Thy sight,"[5]

namely, the sense of wrong done against a person, and that person one who has the greatest claim on our obedience and love ? Remorse is the useless regret at inability to undo the past. Shame would seem to be wholly self-regarding, and to have its roots in wounded self-esteem, self-esteem wounded by a lowering of our own or someone else's opinion of us. Regret at the uncomfortable and unprofitable results of our actions seems to have no moral element in it at all. It is purely economic, and has its roots in expediency. A sense of sin is a sense of unworthiness before God, and of ingratitude to Him, and penitence is

[5] Ps. li. 4.

the child of love. If the most fundamental element of man's relation to God is the sense of the Master-Servant, the Owner-Possessed, relation, the sense of being an unprofitable servant,[6] lost pieces of money[7] still bearing the not altogether obliterated image of the king, may be regarded as the next most fundamental and universal.

Yet this sense of sin, as I have explained elsewhere,[8] is never without its element of hope and encouragement. Sin is something done against love ; but, just because God is Love, pardon and renewal are certain. When the sinner knows God he knows that he is a sinner, but he knows, too, that he can say : " O Lord, I will praise Thee ; though Thou wast angry with me, Thine anger is turned away, and Thou comfortedst me."[9] The sense of being owned by God is, we may believe, based on the essential nature of man, who is a being kept in existence from moment to moment by God's power and will, so that if God were to turn away His face from man for a moment it would be as impossible for him to continue to exist as for

> " Mine image in the glass
> To tarry when myself am gone."

And the sense of sin, of alienation from the source of our true being, is a witness to the real condition of fallen man. But the knowledge that God is Love is something far more intimate. It is the result of *experience of God*, as the knowledge that the sun is bright and warm is the result of experience of the sun. I know nothing so universally true in religion as this, namely, that when the soul has experimental knowledge of God it finds Him to be Love. From the time when God revealed Himself to Abraham, and said : " Fear not, Abram, I am thy shield and thy exceeding great reward,"[10] to the present day, the man who gains direct knowledge of God finds Him loving, benevolent, a source of comfort and well-being.

---

[6] Luke xvii. 10.   [7] Luke xv. 8.
[8] *Our Lord and Saviour*. Longmans, 1928, p. 55–57.
[9] Isaiah xii. 1.   [10] Genesis xv. 1.

I have quoted from the beautiful twelfth chapter of
Isaiah because it is a text that comes readily to one's mind,
but there is hardly a book in the Bible, and hardly a work
dealing with personal experience of religion, from which
it would not be possible to draw evidence of the truth that
God is Love. But neither in this case, nor in any other
where I make any statement about the nature of God, do
I wish to prove it. I quote a text to illustrate my meaning,
and to make my point clear. I want my readers to prove,
or disprove, what I say for themselves. I can imagine few
things which would more surely deepen anyone's spiritual
life than to search Holy Scripture, and devotional literature,
and religious biography, and the experience of men and
women met in daily life, for testimony to this fact that God
is " a God ready to pardon, gracious and merciful, slow to
anger and of great kindness."[11] Indeed Bible study would
grow in interest and in fruitfulness if we read it with the
purpose of finding out what testimony it bears to God's
character, and if we tried to illustrate it from other
sources and let it, in turn, illustrate and explain books and
life.

And one thing which Holy Scripture and the experience
of the saints in all ages, and our own soul's experience,
combine to prove is that though God is Love, His Love for us
is not a weak, easy-going, unexacting thing. The testimony
quoted in the first chapter of this book is true. God is the
best Master in the world ; but He will be Master. When
the soul is still young in the spiritual life, and indeed with
many of us for years and years, the endeavour to walk with
God is marred, from time to time, by the attempt to make
God go our way, instead of our surrendering ourselves to
go His way. Any one who has cultivated the art of self-
knowledge, and has really tried to see himself as he is,
must be conscious that there have been times when he has
tried to get just a little of his own way even with God ; to
pay God His dues but to keep back just a little of the price ;
to persuade God to spare him some part of the needful
discipline. But it is a profound truth that God, Who will
forgive us every bit of the punishment we deserve, will not

[11] Nehemiah ix. 17.

spare us the least tiny portion of the discipline we need. Jesus came to reveal God to us as *Father*; and He is a Father too truly loving to be weakly indulgent. He will be satisfied with nothing but our perfection.

Closely allied with this experience of God as a jealous God—for the attribute we have been considering is that jealousy of which we thought in the first chapter—is experience of God as a holy God. This also is a plain experience, open to all of us. " If I incline unto wickedness with mine heart, the Lord will not hear me," exclaims the psalmist.[12] But he immediately adds : " But God hath heard me, and considered the voice of my prayer. Praised be God who hath not cast out my prayer, nor turned His mercy from me." He finds, by experience, the power that evil has to close the eyes of the soul, and to cut us off from God. But while he owns that this is so, he asserts, in almost the same breath, the reality of his past experience of God and of His goodness. And this fact, that only the pure in heart shall see God, and that holiness is a condition of communion with Him, a thing " without which no man shall see God," can be proved by every one of us, for we all know how angry, selfish, impure thoughts render prayer impossible. Nor is it without significance that of all sins none so shuts the heart to God as hatred, since God is Love. These are truths which, alas, we can all prove.

We prove then for ourselves experimentally that God is holy. But one element of holiness is justice. Now this is an attribute of God which the present age does not care to remember. Many people to-day seem to have persuaded themselves that punishment of sin is an idea alien to a right view of God, and that if men suffer for their sins such retribution is limited to the amount that " natural laws " demand. Neither my own experience, nor that of the human race, seems to bear out this view. When the ancients pictured Nemesis, the goddess of vengeance, as an old, lame, but untiring woman, slow but sure to overtake in the long run, had their thought no foundation in experience ? And the lines :

[12] Ps. lxvi. 16. P. B. version.

Though the mills of God grind slowly, yet they grind exceeding small,
Though with patience He stands waiting, with exactness
grinds He all,

express an idea which can be traced back to the sibylline
oracles of the second century A.D. Robert Browning's
poem, "Halbert and Hob," tells how a father is dragged, on
a bitter snowy night, to the door of his hut by his brutal
son, who means to throw him out into the snow ; and how
the father bids his son pause and relent on the threshold
because he himself, the father, had dragged his father in
the same way, to the same spot, and then relented. The
poem will seem melodramatic and false in sentiment to
many persons. Yet I can vouch for the truth of a story not
wholly unlike it. I was once visiting a sick woman of very
indifferent character, the mother of very unsatisfactory
boys and girls. She was in bed, seriously ill, and was
engaged lamenting the cruelty and ingratitude of her eldest
daughter, who had run away from home and got married,
leaving her mother helpless on a bed of sickness. I have
never been able to explain why I said it, but I suddenly
remarked : " I suppose, Mrs. B——, you were always a
good and dutiful daughter." The woman started violently,
and said : " Who told you ? " I replied : " Nobody has
told me anything. But perhaps you had better tell me."
She then admitted that she had run off to get married,
leaving her own mother ill in bed, and that her mother
never even knew where she was till two months after the
wedding. " Ah, well ! " I said, " God gives us back our
own. I've never known boy or girl yet, who was good to
father or mother, who did not get a reward, nor one who
was bad to father or mother to whom God did not give
back their own." I know that the idea that even in this
life God punishes them that do ill will be repulsive to many.
I wonder if the corresponding truth, that God rewards the
righteous, will prove equally unwelcome to the modern
mind. At any rate I can only record what my own experience leads me to believe. And certainly, in five-and-thirty
years' pretty close and intimate knowledge of young people,

D

I have again and again seen those who have been conspicuously good to their parents—to parents perhaps not
notably deserving of such goodness—conspicuously re-
warded. This, of course, involves a view of Divine providence
which is very unfashionable to-day. We are still so much
under the influence of nineteenth-century thought, which
when not atheistic was often unconsciously deistic,[13] that
the thought of a God who " ordereth all things both in
Heaven and earth " is repulsive to many people. Personally,
I can see no reason for doubting that not a sparrow falls on
the ground without our Father.[14] But we shall have to
discuss the subject of God's providence in the next chapter.

What, then, may we claim that experience teaches us of
God and of man, and of the relations of one to the other ?
It may be helpful to tabulate our conclusions :

(1) There is the Master-Servant, the Owner-Owned, relationship bearing witness to the fact that God created us ;
that from moment to moment He holds us in being ; that
He created us for Himself ; and that in Him all the needs
of our being find satisfaction.

(2) There is the consciousness of sin, bearing witness to
some deep-seated corruption of our nature, some alienation
of unregenerate man from his Maker.

(3) There is the direct apprehension of God as Good, so
that to have any direct experience of Him at all is to
experience Him as Love.

(4) There is the experience, which every year of life
deepens and confirms, that this love is no weak affability
and good-nature, but a love strong and exacting, refusing
to be satisfied with anything short of our moral perfection.

(5) There is the proof of God's holiness supplied by the
way in which sin drops a shutter, as it were, between the
soul and God.

---

[13] The *atheist*, as all my readers will know, denies the existence of
God. The *deist* admitted the existence of a God but put Him
altogether outside the world, as a clockmaker is outside, and apart
from, the watch he has made. And so they, rightly from their
point of view, denied miracles, and an active providence of God in
human affairs.

[14] Matt. x. 29.

(6) There is the witness of human history, and of our own experience, that God is a God of justice, one of whom we may aptly say : " The Lord of recompenses shall surely requite."[15]

Now there are, of course, many other points in the relationship between God and His creatures on which it might be helpful to touch. Few, I should suppose, can have thought much about God's dealings with men without being struck by the long-suffering of God, and His patience. And a whole volume might be written on the text : " I am the Lord ; I change not " ;[16] for there are few more arresting experiences than to recognize the strange similarity—I had almost said identity—of God's dealings with some East London boy, or Lancashire weaver, or woman in a back street here in Salford, and His dealings with Abraham, or Moses, or Mary Magdalene. And along with this unchangeableness of God there is something for which I can find no other word than His grand simplicity. The means man takes to attain his ends are often so tortuous, so complicated, so clever. And then we see God's ways and they are direct, simple, and plain. But I do not want to discuss these, and a score of other points, in detail. Rather let the reader make his own the words of the psalmist : " I will meditate also of all Thy work, and talk of Thy doings," and he will find that there is no subject of meditation so inexhaustible as God.

But there is one aspect of the relationship of God to man, and of man to God, which must be touched on before this chapter closes. Many persons—but, as I most firmly believe, always those who know nothing about it—declare the desire to rest in and on God, and find fulness of life in absolute surrender to Him, to be merely the cry of the weak, the cowardly, and the beaten man. Nietzsche gave prominence to this view when he described Christianity as " the revolt of all things that crawl on their bellies against everything that is lofty."[17] But he was neither the first nor

---

[15] Jeremiah li. 56.   [16] Malachi iii. 6.
[17] " The Antichrist," p. 187 of *The Twilight of the Idols.* See also : *The Will to Power, passim*, for descriptions of Christians as " the wretched, the bungled, and the botched."

the last to take this view, though he expressed it with
more violence than others. Matthew Arnold apparently
thought the attitude of mind described in his sonnet,
beginning :

> Foil'd by our fellow-men, depress'd, outworn,
> We leave the brutal world to take its way,

an attitude typical of many, if not all, Christian people.
And some years ago an article appeared in an ecclesiastical
weekly, now extinct, lamenting the failure of the Church
to attract really manly men, describing men who to-day
take their religion seriously as " weak creatures," and dis-
missing the whole question of prayer as mere sentimentality
and a weak-kneed begging from God for things one should
do for oneself.   Now there are few texts in the Bible more
obviously true than the one which says : " The devil is a
liar."[18] By this I mean that the things which the worldly
and irreligious man says about religion, and firmly believes,
and accepts as so obvious as to need no proof, are almost
invariably so untrue that one minute's serious reflection
would prevent any sensible person from repeating them.
To take one single, glaring example. St. Paul, in his great
list of the fruits of the spirit, puts joy second only to love.[19]
The world is sure that religious people are sad, unhappy,
sour-faced people making themselves and others miserable.
People who hear the charge made assent to it, and repeat it,
as they assent to any other oft-repeated fallacy, as, for
instance, that summers now are not as hot as they used to
be when we were young, or that we always had " good old-
fashioned snowy Christmas days " twenty years ago.
Whereas, if any one would take the trouble to take a pencil
and a piece of paper, and to make a list of those persons of
the reality of whose religion he is most sure, and then
ask himself the plain question : " Are these people either
themselves unhappy, or the cause of unhappiness in others ?
Or do they, on the contrary, seem to enjoy life as much as,
and more than, the average of their fellow-men ? " he would
never again be able to hear the charge of joylessness brought

[18] John viii. 44.   [19] Gal. v. 22.

against religion and religious people without scoffing. But of all the obvious lies invented by the Father of Lies, surely the most bare-faced and absurd is the charge that religion either attracts the cowardly or diminishes man's vital powers, whether of body, mind, or soul. Indeed, there are some things so obvious that I am almost ashamed to stress them. They are :

(1) That at school or at the university, in the warehouse or workshop, in the army or the navy—in short, in every condition of life—the man who sticks to and practises his religion needs and displays an iron courage, of which the man who simply drifts, and is willing to take the tone of his environment, knows nothing.

(2) That so far from religion attracting persons of low vitality and enervated powers, there is no way of presenting religion which is so effective in attracting converts as to present it as an adventure, a high endeavour, a thing taxing every nerve and making claim on every power.

(3) That the result of an entire submission to God is not the loss of one's personality, but the enormous quickening of it in every possible way. When Christ said : " Whosoever will save his life shall lose it, and whosoever will lose his life for my sake shall find it," [20] He stated a truth which hundreds of thousands in every age have proved by experience. Christ comes into our being that we may have life, and have it more abundantly. [21]

(4) That this fulness of life is no mere heightening and quickening of the emotions. It is a very real, definite, and measurable increase of all the powers of a man's personality. If I had to say what was the truth most firmly and clearly established in my mind by more than forty years' work among the poor and uneducated, and especially among young people, I should say that it was the truth that there is no educative process comparable to religion, nor anything which so develops the best powers of mind and spirit. Rain, fresh air, and sunlight are not more unquestionably good for a growing plant than God is good for a growing boy or girl.

I believe modern psychologists regard fear as the cause

[20] Matt. xvi. 25.   [21] John x. 10.

of most of the weaknesses, failures, and inhibitions from which we suffer. If that is so anything which cures fear makes for fulness of life. Well, a German author writes : " The compensation for the loss of that sense of personal independence which man so unwillingly gives up, is the disappearance of all *fear* from one's life, the quite indescribable and inexplicable feeling of an inner *security*, which one can only experience, but which, once it has been experienced, one can never forget."[22]

The conclusion, then, at which we have arrived in this chapter is that man needs God, finds in Him the entire satisfaction of all his wants, and only finds his true existence in Him. Man and God may truly be said to fit one another as the key fits the lock. " For of Him, and through Him, and to Him, are all things ; to Whom be glory for ever. Amen."[23]

[22] C. H. Hilty ; quoted in Wm. James' " The Varieties of Religious Experience," Lecture on Saintliness.
[23] Rom. xi. 36.

CHAPTER V

IN the last chapter we have, implicitly if not directly, asserted such a relationship between man and God, and such a view of Divine providence, as will seem to many people inconsistent with modern scientific views. Is it possible, in these days, to believe that God's "never-failing providence ordereth all things in Heaven and earth"?[1] Even if we say yes to that question, do not modern views about the uniformity and universality of natural law compel us to reject the notion of special interventions, on God's part, to guide, correct, or keep individuals, and must we not limit very closely the spheres in which prayer can be efficacious? Are we not, in short, compelled to say: "God indeed orders and directs everything, but He does it, we must believe, by a process of unvarying natural law, and all so-called 'special providences' are a delusion."

At the very outset let us recognize that, even among persons with a very true religion, and a sincere love of God, the answers given to this question will vary. A well-known clergyman, still living, for whom I have not merely a great respect, but a sincere affection, once told me that if he believed in the "fussy providence" (the expression was his) in which I seemed to believe, life would be perfectly intolerable to him. I replied that unless I could believe in a God to Whom I could say: "Thou art about my path, and about my bed, and spiest out all my ways,"[2] I should not care to go on living any longer. If then I seem to claim, in this connection, more than the reader can believe, or perhaps even wish to believe, he must remember that I am necessarily stating my own views, and that others have as much right

---

[1] Collect for Eighth Sunday after Trinity. [2] Ps. cxxxix. 2.

to theirs as I have to mine. So let us try to get to grips
with the question.

Firstly, what is the evidence on the matter ? What
reason have we for accepting or rejecting the belief that God
interferes in human affairs, guiding, directing, and over-ruling
them ? I wrote, in 1914, in a little tract for soldiers, that
I could imagine a man, uncertain whether to spend his
holidays at Blackpool or in the Isle of Man, deciding the
matter by spinning a coin, and the coin coming down
" heads," for Blackpool, and not " tails " for the Isle of
Man, because God had planned, before time began, that
he should meet at Blackpool some man who would change
the whole course of his life. Now against this view friends
have urged two objections, (a) that it destroys man's free-
will and makes man a mere puppet of fate ; and (b) that
whether true or false it is necessarily incapable of proof.
Let us consider these two points.

(a) I do not think any man could be a more convinced
believer in Free Will than I am. It is intimately bound up
with all that I most firmly believe, and the objections
brought against the doctrine appear to me to be altogether
rooted and grounded in misapprehensions and confusions
of thought. But I cannot argue the question here. I have
stated my views on the Free Will question in the fourth
chapter of my book *The Problem of Evil*,[3] and neither
fifteen years of further thought on the matter—for the book,
though published in 1920, was written in 1913—nor the
experiences of the Great War, have in any way modified
the conclusions there stated. But I do not think that the
fullest belief in the freedom of man's will need modify our
belief in the reality of God's providence. When we assert
belief in the freedom of man's will, we assert our belief that
he can choose between various alternatives, and that such
choice is a real and determining factor in his actions. But
we do not assert that a man will always be able to realize
the objects of his choice. A man's choice is free ; his actions
are often hampered and modified by circumstances. An
illustration may make the point clear. When I was defend-
ing the doctrine of Free Will in an ecclesiastical weekly, a

[3] Longmans, 1920.

young mechanic wrote me a furious letter asking how he could be said to be free. He desired, he said, knowledge, opportunity to develop his intellectual powers, and the advantages of leisure, travel, and intercourse with the best minds. And he had been compelled to leave school at fourteen, and to work, ever since then, for long hours at a dull and depressing trade which offered no opportunities of self-development or of success. I wrote, as sympathetically as I could, to point out that I had never claimed that all man's *actions* were free. It was the freedom of the *Will* for which I contended. While we need not be surprised that the explanation did not satisfy the young man, I hope my readers will grasp the point. Man's character, and his actions throughout life, are the fruit of two interacting factors, his will and his environment. And these factors, both necessary for the final result, run, so to speak, at right angles the one to the other, like the warp and the woof of a piece of cloth, and so often seem to be at cross purposes. And among the factors which go to make up man's environment the chief is the providence of God " in Whom we live, and move, and have our being."[4] But this does not prevent man from being a creature possessed of free will.

(*b*) If we turn to the other objection, and ask what positive evidence there is for God's interference in man's life, our answer must obviously run on different lines. It will not be a question of abstract reasoning, but of concrete examples. And here, as in all such cases, that evidence will carry most weight which the reader collects for himself. But this I would say. One very common fruit of a deepened spiritual life, and more extended religious experience, seems to be the growing conviction that one's life has been ordered and directed from the first, and that God has graciously used and overruled even one's sins and failures to forward His purposes of love. The word of the Lord came to the prophet Jeremiah : " Before I formed thee in the belly I knew thee ; and before thou camest forth out of the womb I sanctified thee, and I ordained thee a prophet unto the nations."[5] St. Paul contrasts the days of his youth and

[4] Acts xvii. 28.   [5] Jeremiah i. 5.

early manhood with the time "when it pleased God, who separated me from my mother's womb, and called me by His grace, to reveal His Son in me."[6]   There is, of course, the expression of exactly the same conviction in numbers of religious biographies.   One of the most striking that comes to my mind at the moment is the story of the "Girl forced to be a nun," quoted in full in *The Nuns of Port Royal* : *As Seen in their Own Narratives*, by M. E. Lowndes.[7] However psychologists may explain it, the fact remains that the girl felt herself "forced," by a power altogether opposed to her own desires and volitions, towards an end in which she ultimately found entire peace and happiness. There is a very beautiful expression of this sense of God's habitual guidance throughout life in Joseph Addison's poem, "When all Thy mercies, O my God." It should be read in its entirety, as printed in *The Book of Praise*,[8] or in the *Spectator*, in number 453, where it originally appeared, and not in hymn-books like *Hymns, Ancient and Modern*, which omit many verses.   But, at the risk of being tedious, I will repeat what I have already said, namely, that in this case, and in all similar cases, that evidence is the most convincing which we collect for ourselves, not from books but from life, from our own soul's experience and the experience of men and women we have known.   And that evidence, quite inconclusive to some minds, will convince those who have had experiences of their own of the kind described, that God's providence is the most real and intimate thing in life.

There is one objection, which it may be worth while to examine at this point, namely, the objection that, in view of what modern science has revealed about the universe, man must be recognized as too insignificant a creature to engage the attention of the Creator.   Of course, much has been said about the insignificance of man ever since Tennyson wrote the line :

"What is it all but the trouble of ants in the glare of a million million of suns ? "

[6] Gal. i. 15 and 16.   [7] Henry Frowde, 1909.
[8] Golden Treasury Series.   Macmillan.

But that whole position fails to appeal to me in the least. Grant that our stellar system contains as many millions of stars as you like ; admit that there are other systems as big lying beyond it in the depths of space ; talk as much as you will of star systems whose light takes a million years to reach us, and of suns many million times as large as our own sun, and radiating ten thousand times as much energy. What does it all amount to ? Size, that is all. But to claim that therefore man is insignificant and unworthy of the Creator's attention seems to me like arguing that, in the case of a fire, a mother should hasten to rescue the ash-bin rather than the baby, on the ground that it weighs more. Values are not decided by the scales and the yard measure. Of course, if this universe is the product of pure chance, and if the course of evolution is without purpose or meaning, then man is not the purpose of a development which is, *ex hypothesi*, purposeless. But if we believe that there is any meaning and purpose in the cosmic process, where can that meaning and purpose be sought if not in man ? To put the matter as bluntly as possible, if God is not interested in man, in what can we suppose that He is interested ? Some people may prefer to adopt a frankly agnostic attitude in face of this question, and say that we cannot conceive what the purpose of the universe can be, or what in it the Creator can value. That does not seem to me a very rational position, nor does it prove itself in practice a position fruitful in moral or intellectual fruits. But if we find it impossible to surrender the belief that life has some meaning, then surely that meaning can be sought in connection with nothing other than human beings. People say that it is impossible to suppose that a universe which has existed for untold billions of years, and a world which has been evolving for a period calculated by physicists as some multiple, " probably more than three and less than ten," of a thousand million years, can find its purpose expressed in a race of men which has existed at the most for a quarter of a million years. Can all this space, they ask, can all these unnumbered suns, can all this ceaseless working through infinite time, be for us and our race ? The mountain is in labour, the mouse it brings forth is indeed ridiculous ! To this I have always replied that this is, in fact, just exactly the way in which we do find nature working. The female cod spawns a hundred million eggs that one may come to perfection. The oak scatters a thousand acorns that one new oak may grow. If nature desires to see her crown and glory, man, might we not expect her to throw a million suns into space that one may carry a planet fit for her darling to develop upon ? Recently, to my delight, I have come across that argument, in almost those words, in Professor Eddington's profoundly interesting book, *The Nature of the Physical World*. And I was glad also to come across the following sentence on the subject of the possibility of other worlds being inhabited. The Professor says :

"I do not think that the whole purpose of the Creation has been staked on the one planet where we live ; and in the long run we cannot deem ourselves the only race that has been or will be gifted with the mystery of consciousness. But I feel inclined to claim that *at the present time* our race is supreme ; and not one of the profusion of stars in their myriad clusters looks down on scenes comparable to those that are passing beneath the rays of the sun."

And supposing that the Professor is wrong, and that there are now, in distant parts of space, worlds inhabited by conscious beings ; what then ? The most outstanding fact that modern science has established is that the universe is indeed a uni-verse ; that it is, that is to say, all of one piece. The stars are all made of the same materials, they are all of one pattern, they all pass, with almost pedantic uniformity, through the same course of evolution, so that every star, it seems, has been, is, or will be, what our own sun now is, a " dwarf of the G class." The chief exception to this wide generalization seems to be that a rare accident was needed to endow our sun with his retinue of planets, and perhaps another as rare to make our earth a fit place for the evolution of life. But if the professors are wrong in what they tell us on this last point we may be sure that if on other worlds there are conscious beings, then, though they may differ from men as widely as giant saurians differ from humming-birds, they will have this in common with us : that they are products of organic evolution. They will be, that is to say, like us, intelligent animals, not godlike creatures. So the answer which modern science gives to our question : " If God is not interested in human beings, in what is He interested ? " though given tentatively and on the balance of probabilities, is that " Our race is supreme." Man may well be humble in the presence of his Maker. I cannot see that there is anything else, from electron to star-cluster, with which nature confronts him before which he need bow. For surely a child that can know, love, and choose the good is of more value than the stellar galaxy.

When, then, we have cleared our minds of false ideas as to what God can and cannot do, and what He is or is not likely to do, and what we think He ought or ought not to do —and it is extraordinary how many people allow their religion to be hampered and spoilt by the remains of the shoddy philosophizing of the last century, misconceptions as to God, moral freedom, and immortality which may justly be classed as oppositions of science *falsely so called*—we can give due weight to the evidence of direct religious experience. And the universal and absolutely unvarying witness which direct experience of God yields is that He cares, He is interested, He loves. It would be impossible even to begin to quote the mass of evidence to this truth which the religious autobiography of the whole race supplies. But one piece of, so to speak, negative evidence is most interesting. Nothing so stirs Nietzsche's indignation, nothing so inflames his hatred against Christianity, as the way in which the sense of their value in the eyes of God leads " paltry people "[9] to behave as if they mattered, to be brave, and calm, and strong.

But we must not be content to rest on the evidence of others. Every one should be constantly striving to increase his experience of God. And the way to that is prayer. Now, of course, volumes have been written, and will be written, about prayer. But really the whole philosophy of prayer is contained in two texts. They are our Blessed

[9] Works, *passim*, but see specially *The Will to Power*, Vol. I., pp. 145–148, Sections 175 and 176.

Lord's words : " When ye pray, say *Our Father*,"[10] and
St. Paul's words : " Though He be not far from every one
of us : For in Him we live, and move, and have our being."[11]

Let us consider our Lord's words first. When He bids us,
when we pray, say " Our Father," He does not, I am sure,
mean to order us to use one set form of words every time
we pray. No, indeed, what He meant was : " When you
pray, draw near to God as to an infinitely wise, patient, and
loving Father. Never for one moment allow any thought
of God, which is inconsistent with the thought of Him as
Father, to cross your mind."

It is wonderful how a steady refusal to think of God as
anything except a wise and loving Father sweeps away
the difficulties about prayer with which men so often
trouble themselves and others. Let me take an illustration.
Once, when taking a Mission in a small mill-town in Yorkshire, I held dinner-hour services on a piece of open ground
close to three large dye-works. The men from the dye-
works, and from other neighbouring works and mills,
gathered in good numbers, and were invited to ask questions
at the close of the address. One day, when the address had
been on prayer, a man said : " I don't see how you make
out the case for prayer. If God is as wise as you say, He
must know best what is good for us ; and if He is the loving
Father you say He is, He will give it to us without our
asking for it."

" Nay, old lad," I replied, " that's just where you are
wrong. If He is the loving Father I think He is, He won't
give us what is best till we learn to ask for it."

Then I told him the following story. A short time before
I had been having tea with a married friend. His little
boy of six had snatched at the cake. I was just going to
pass it to him, when his father said : " No ! don't give it
to him. Let him learn to ask for it properly."

Was this because he did not love the child ? Surely not.
It was because he did really love him and knew that good
manners are a better thing for a little boy than a piece of
sugar-cake. If, then, real knowledge of God, and the power
to hold intimate communion with Him, is a thing more to

[10] Luke xi. 2.   [11] Acts xvii. 27 and 28.

be desired than anything else in life, if God Himself is better than any, and all, of His gifts He may well withhold lesser blessings from us if so we may be led on to learn the difficult art of prayer. So too with all the questions men raise as to why our prayers are not always answered, or at any rate not answered as we expect and desire ; as to why God's ways puzzle us so often ; and as to why different men seem to receive such unequal treatment at God's hands. All these difficulties can be solved in the light of the Fatherhood of God. It is now many years since, as a curate at Leeds, I used to stop on my way down from the Leeds Infirmary to the Parish Church Clergy House, after the late evening service for the nurses, to listen to atheist speakers in the Town Hall Square. One night a speaker said : " If God were a Heavenly Father, as the parsons tell us, He'd treat us all alike." " Oh, surely not ! " I said. " You seem to be confusing a Heavenly Father with a Heavenly Police Magistrate. The magistrate has to treat us all alike. The glory of a Father is that He can love all His children equally and treat them all differently." Surely that is true. A wise father will check the rash and forward, and encourage the timid and diffident. He will be strict with the extravagant and loose-principled, and indulgent with the careful and trustworthy. And still his treatment of his children may be no indication of which he loves best, and if he is an exceptionally wise and good man he may succeed in loving them all alike just when, and because, he is treating them all differently.

But what help can we draw, in thinking out for ourselves a philosophy of prayer, from St. Paul's declaration that indeed God is not far from us, but that we live in Him ? Why we get an answer, ready to our hand, to the objections of those who say that God rules this world by " natural law," and that all prayers to God which ask for any inter-ference with natural processes, such as prayers for rain, or for good weather, for protection at sea, or restoration in times of illness, are vain. Some people allow value to prayers for the sick—apparently on the ground that the act of prayer, by the sick person, or the knowledge that he is being prayed for, by others, may favourably affect the sick person's mental state, and so prove beneficial—but deny the value of prayers for rain or fine weather. Thus the late William James writes :[12] " As regards prayers for the sick, if any medical fact can be considered to stand firm, it is that in certain environments prayer may contribute to recovery, and should be encouraged as a therapeutic measure. Being a normal factor of moral health in the person, its omission would be deleterious. The case of the weather is different. Notwithstanding the recency of the opposite belief, every one now knows that droughts and storms follow from physical antecedents, and that moral appeals cannot avert them." Here prayer is clearly regarded only from the point of view of its *direct effect on man* ; its effect, if any, on God is ignored or denied ; and that, too, on supposedly scientific grounds. But, if I may adopt the Professor's own form of words, I would say that *notwith-standing the recency of the opposite belief* Professor James, on this point at least, is already out of date. Dr. F. R. Tennant, speaking at the 1924 Conference of Modern Churchmen, at Oxford, said : " If prayer for the control of the physical was to be ruled out, it must be on ethical, not on scientific, grounds." Put bluntly, this means that a man may, if he likes, argue that God *ought* not to answer man's petitions, either because it is unworthy of His dignity to be moved by man's prayers or because He ought to treat us all alike— both of which contentions, however, are obviously ruled out by the thought of God as *a Father*—but he must not argue that science proves that God cannot, or at least does not, interfere, for as a matter of fact science proves nothing of the sort. Can we make the point at issue clear to ordinary men and women, and make it clear in a few words ? I think so. Men often argue that God has created this world, and governs it by fixed laws which man can, at any rate partly, discover and understand. Now a watchmaker who, having made and wound up a watch, had to be continually altering it, now pushing the hands on a bit and now pushing them back, would merely show himself a clumsy workman. So, too, they argue, with God. He has no need to be constantly modifying and altering His own laws ,and this hour-to-hour,

[12] " The Varieties of Religious Experience." Lecture XIX.

and moment-to-moment, supervision of His universe is unnecessary and unworthy of Him. But to conceive of God and His universe as of a clockmaker and a clock is, as we saw in the last chapter, to fall into the old deistic error of the eighteenth century. God is not a Being outside, and apart from, His universe. That universe, and we human beings who are parts of the universe and its children, are *in* God, and He in His universe and in us. No analogy between God and anything other than God can ever be quite perfect. But if we want an analogy to illustrate the relationship of God to the universe, the analogy of a man's spirit to his body will be a better one than that of a man (say a clockmaker) to what he has mechanically fashioned (say a watch). It is easy for any one to see how this affects the question of God's intervention, in human affairs, in answer to prayer. Suppose I am anxious to get this page of manuscript finished before I go to bed. I look up and see the clock on my mantelpiece, and notice that the hands stand at a quarter to eleven. No one believes that, without moving from my chair, I can by a mere act of will cause them to stand at a quarter to nine. I and the clock are two mutually distinct things, external to one another. But suppose my desire is not to alter the position of the hands of the clock, which is on the other side of the room, but to change the position in which I am sitting, which feels a little cramped, and to do so by *altering the position of my legs* crossing, one over the other. No one would be the least surprised at such a change being effected by my bare act of will.[13] But then my mind and my body, even if from some points of view they are mutually distinct things, are certainly not external to one another. If, then, God has indeed such a relationship to the world as justifies us in saying that we live and have our being in Him, it is clearly not more impossible for Him to interfere in human affairs

[13] When I say that no one would feel any surprise at my changing the position of my legs *merely because I want to,* I say what is obviously true. I do not mean that there is therefore no mystery in the matter. The relation of mind to body and body to mind, and the question how an act of will can issue in the movement of a material body, are two of the most insoluble problems in philosophy. See *Body and Mind,* by Wm. McDougall. Methuen, 1911.

E

than for a man to lift his hand. No matter how we may
understand that very question-begging phrase " contrary to
natural law," it is no more contrary to natural law for God
to send rain in answer to prayer than it is for a man at the
dinner-table to pass the salt at the request of the person
sitting next him.

I expect the reader will advance two objections. He will
say : " But, firstly, there certainly is an order of nature
and an appearance of regularity in natural phenomena,
which suggests *law* and not *arbitrary acts of will*. And,
secondly, if what you suggest is true, science is impossible.'
These two objections are worth considering.

Firstly, we may unhesitatingly admit, or rather I should
say we must strongly assert, that there is an order of nature,
and an appearance of regularity in natural phenomena.
But this order, we may believe, is a moral, not a mechanical,
one. When I say that my watch is absolutely dependable,
I am asserting a fact due to mechanical causes. The watch
cannot deceive me, nor upset my whole day, by capricious
variations in its behaviour. When I say of a friend that he
is absolutely dependable, I am asserting a fact due to moral
causes. My friend *will not* deceive me, nor upset my whole
day, by capricious variations in his behaviour. So surely
the reliability and dependableness of nature reflects the
character of God, and is due to moral causes at the basis of
all reality rather than to any mechanical necessity. I have
heard the late Dr. Moorhouse, second bishop of Manchester,
tell a story that illustrates this idea. Late at night, in a
small Lancashire mill-town, the local atheist was holding
forth to a small crowd of men. At last he said, pointing to
the clock in the church tower : " Come ! if there's a God
I'll challenge Him. Let him stop that clock now, before it
strikes ten, and I'll believe in Him." A voice from the
crowd replied : " Eh ! lad," it said, "dost tha think God
A'mighty's got no more sense than to make us all late for
t'mill to-morrow morning to convert a saphead like thee ? "
God is not likely to bewilder His children, and render vain
the toil of men of science, by arbitrary and capricious inter-
ferences with the regular order of nature. On the contrary,
a modern writer on astronomy says, very beautifully as it

seems to me : " It has been said that the Almighty must smile on scientific research, or He would not have filled the universe with so many clues to its character."[14] We pay a man no compliment when we say of him that you never know what he will do next, and that it is impossible to depend on him from moment to moment. So we should not be honouring, but rather dishonouring, God if we denied the existence of an order in nature. But God is not limited by His own laws. He is free in the universe of His own creation.

As to the objection that if God interferes in human affairs science becomes impossible there is a twofold reply. Firstly, we may say that the fact that man certainly *behaves as if he possessed Free Will* (I put it this way since the most convinced determinist will hardly deny that man behaves as if moved by the impulses of an unfettered volition) does not render science impossible. And secondly, we may say that the whole attitude of mind of men of science towards the subject of natural law has undergone a radical change during the last five and twenty years. What would the master of science of the last quarter of the nineteenth century have said to the following paragraph by one of our leading scientific and philosophical thinkers ?

" It is *possible* that the desire for rational explanation may be carried too far. This is suggested by some remarks by Eddington, in his book on *Space, Time, and Gravitation* (p. 200). The theory of relativity has shown that most of traditional dynamics, which was supposed to contain scientific laws, really consisted of conventions as to measurement, and was strictly analogous to the ' great law ' that there are always three feet in a yard. In particular, this applies to the conservation of energy. This makes it plausible to suppose that every apparent law of nature which strikes us as reasonable is not really a law of nature, but a concealed convention, plastered on to nature by our love of what we, in our arrogance, choose to consider rational."[15]

[14] *Modern Astrophysics*, by Herbert Dingle, F.R.A.S. Collins & Co., 1924, p. 25.
[15] *The A B C of Atoms*, by the Hon. Bertrand Russell. Kegan Paul, 1924, p. 170.

So, then, we may say that if the spiritual experience of religious men of all nations, and in all ages, leads to belief in a God Who cares, Who hears prayer, Who interferes in man's affairs to guide, to protect, and to reward, there is nothing in the teachings of science which need make us deny this experience or lead us to refuse it its due place in our general scheme of reality.

One thing remains to be discussed in connection with prayer and the miraculous. When all other objections to the idea that God intervenes in human affairs, hearing and answering prayer, have been met and answered, one objection still remains. God, we believe, is infinite Wisdom. Can we then believe that He alters His plans in answer to our prayers ? Would the experienced head of a great firm alter his plans on the advice of the junior office-boy ? Would Napoleon have recast his strategy to meet the views of a raw recruit ? Can we think that the prayer of such " grass-hoppers " as we are can modify the plans of Him Who " sitteth upon the circle of the earth . . . stretcheth out the heavens as a curtain, and spreadeth them out as a tent to dwell in " ?[16]

I am sorry to have to labour the point, but the fallacy here is just this, that we are *not* thinking of God as a *Father*, but as the head of a firm or the commander of an army. Think of a wise and loving father. He says to his wife : " I'm sorry I can't send Fred to Cambridge. He is so reckless, and lazy, and extravagant, and untrustworthy. I dare not risk it. He must just go into the business where I can keep an eye on him." Then something, the disgrace of one of his wild companions, a severe illness, or what not, sobers the lad. He speaks frankly and earnestly to his father, admitting and lamenting his past faults, and promising amendment. That night the father says to his wife : " I've decided to send Fred to college. He spoke to me to-day, and pleased me very much. I am sure he will make good." Do you say that the father has changed his mind or his plans ? Surely not. It is the boy who has changed, not the father. The father always meant one thing, and desired one thing, the boy's highest good. It is

[16] Isaiah xl. 22.

a change in the lad that has made possible to-day the good which was impossible yesterday. I think the change wrought by prayer is often, perhaps always, a change not in God, but in us. Our prayer may make it possible for God to bless us, or those we pray for, as He could not have blessed if we had not prayed.

CHAPTER VI

GOD, AND A WORLD OF PAIN AND SUFFERING

WE have now come to a stage in our argument where we must face a question which is the most difficult, from the point of view of theory, and the most important, from the point of view of practice, of any question in religion or theology. I mean, of course, the question of pain and suffering. Religion has been defined, in this book, as a disinterested delight in God for His own sake. How is it possible to delight in God when so many things, which force themselves on our attention every day of our lives, suggest that He is cruel, capricious, and unmerciful ? I have declared that in those rare and blessed moments when we have direct experience of God, we experience Him as wholly *good*, and that to *know God*, as distinct from merely *knowing about God*, is to know Him as *Love*. But how can we set these subjective impressions, which psychologists explain in so many different ways, against the grim witness of natural science and of human history ? Man's story, from the dawn of history, and as far back into the gloom of prehistory as the eye can pierce, seems to be little else than a record of blood, tears, and sweat. And when we turn from human history to what is generally called natural history, we see little but suffering, struggle, and death.

I think it is the duty of Christian apologists to face these things. Atheist writers and speakers make full use of them, and we ought to be prepared to answer their arguments. History has usually been written in such a manner that our eyes are fixed on the glories and triumphs of the kings and conquerors to the complete exclusion of the sufferings and miseries of common people. But it is of the common people that I want to think. One of the early cuneiform inscriptions, recording the victories of an Assyrian monarch, reads :

" Before me were fruitful fields and vineyards, behind me solitude and death."[1] We read of the marvels of the Babylon of Nebuchadnezzar, of its walls three hundred feet high, and broad enough at the top for six chariots to drive abreast on them; of the temple of Bel, built on a base two hundred yards square and reaching a height of six hundred feet; of the hanging gardens and the other marvels of the city. But what of the wretched slaves, deported from all countries of the known world, who groaned and sweated under the lash to build these things? The majesty of the Pharaohs lives for us still in the pyramids. I do not want to see them. I think I should still hear, as I looked at them, the crack of the oppressor's whip and the cries of the oppressed. What shall we say of the misery of whole families torn from their homes and sold into slavery by the conquerors of classic times? Here is a passage from Ward Fowler's *Social Life at Rome in the Age of Cicero*."[2]

" After the campaign of Pydna and the overthrow of the Macedonian kingdom, Æmilius Paullus, one of the most humane of Romans, sold into slavery, under orders of the senate, 150,000 free inhabitants of communities in Epirus which had sided with Perseus in the war. After the war with the Cimbri and Teutones 90,000 of the latter and 60,000 of the former are said to have been sold; and though the numbers may be open to suspicion, as they amount again to 150,000, the fact of an enormous capture is beyond question. Cæsar, like Æmilius Paullus, one of the most humane of Romans, tells us himself that on a single occasion, the capture of the Aduatuci, he sold 53,000 prisoners on the spot. And of course every war, whether great or small, while it diminished the free population by slaughter, pestilence, or capture, added to the number of slaves."

Add to the above two further quotations from the same writer :

" In Italy itself, where there was no police protection until Augustus took the matter in hand, kidnapping was by no means unknown ; . . . and many a traveller disappeared in this way and passed the rest of his life in a slave-prison."[3]

[1] I quote from memory.   [2] Macmillan, 1908, p. 207.
[3] *Loc. cit.*, p. 209.

And again :

"No Latin poet of that age shows any real sympathy with captives or with slaves, except, perhaps, Virgil in *Æn.* vii. 333.[4]

If we add to the accounts we possess of slavery in the ancient world the history of negro slavery, " that monstrous sum of all imaginable villainies," as John Wesley called it, what is the sum total of human misery due to slavery alone ?

What was the condition of the majority of mankind during the dark ages that followed the break-up of the Roman Empire ? This is how M. Funck-Brentano opens his volume on " The Middle Ages " in *The National History of France*,[5] of which he is the general editor:

"The night of the ninth century. . . . What is its course ? Dimly the records give a glimpse of a people scattered and without guidance. The Barbarians have broken through the ramparts. The Saracen invasions have spread in successive waves over the South. The Hungarians swarm over the Eastern provinces. ' These strangers,' writes Richer, ' gave themselves over to the most cruel outrages ; they sacked town and village, and laid waste the fields. They burned down the churches and then departed with a crowd of captives, and no one said them nay.' "

What miseries for generation after generation of men, over a whole continent, lie behind these words.

Here is a brief description of the " harrying of the North in 1069 " by William the Conqueror, from Mr. H. W. C. Davis' *England under the Normans and Angevins.*[6]

"In Yorkshire, where there was less time (*i.e.* less time than across the Tees) to learn and to forestall his plans, every village through which he passed became a scene of massacre. A few miserable refugees lurked in the hills and supported existence on the flesh of horses, dogs, and cats. Others sold themselves

[4] Note, p. 208.
[5] *The National History of France.* Edited by M. Funck-Brentano, 6 vols. English translation, Heinemann.
[6] *A History of England*, 6 vols. Edited by C. W. C. Oman. Methuen, 1905.

into slavery; ' they bowed their heads for meat in the evil
days,' to quote the grim expression of a contemporary
document.''

Has any one ever tried to estimate the sum of human
misery due to the Crusades; to the occupation of the
Netherlands under the Duke of Alva ; to the Thirty Years'
War in Germany; to the Fronde;[7] to the campaigns of
Frederick the Great, on whose head, Macaulay says, must
rest " all the blood which was shed in a war which raged
during many years and in every quarter of the globe, the
blood of the column of Fontenoy, the blood of the moun-
taineers who were slaughtered at Culloden " ; to the wars
of Napoleon; to the Great War of 1914-18 ? I am not
thinking only, or indeed chiefly, of the men who died on
the battlefields. But what of the orphans and widows,
what of the peasants whose homes were burnt and whose
fields were ravaged, what of quiet families, living peaceably
in their habitations, brought to sudden ruin ?

And when we have turned away our eyes from the
dreadful spectre of war, there are still the questions of
religious persecutions, of witch hunts, of inhuman legal
punishments.[8] Burns' lines :

> Man's inhumanity to man
> Makes countless thousands mourn,

are true, but no truer than the title of the poem from which
they are taken, *Man was made to Mourn*.

But while we remember the sufferings of men due to the
inhumanity of their fellow-creatures, what shall we say of
natural catastrophes ? Who can read, unmoved, the records
of volcanic eruptions, of Krakatoa, which exploded in 1883
and despatched tidal waves to drown 36,000 people on
neighbouring coasts ; or of Mont Pelée, which overwhelmed
the town of Saint Pierre on Ascension Day, 1902, and
destroyed 40,000 people in a few hours, with every cir-
cumstance of agony and terror ? What of the horrors of

---

[7] See *La Misère au temps de la Fronde*. Fieullet, Paris.
[8] For all these matters see Lecky's *The Rise and Influence of
Rationalism in Europe*, *passim*.

earthquakes: of the Lisbon earthquake in 1755, with its toll of 60,000 lives; or that of Calabria in 1783, with a death roll of 30,000; of Messina in 1908, with its 100,000 victims of Kansu, in China, where between 100,000 and 200,000 perished in 1920; or of the Japanese catastrophe in 1923, when 142,000 perished? Nor are the mere numbers the most appalling feature of such disasters. Writing of the Japanese earthquake of 1923 one authority says: " It is said that 32,000 persons were burned to death in the Military Clothing Yard at Tokyo. Many more perished in pools of water that boiled with the heat of the conflagration."[9] It is unnecessary to dwell on the misery caused by plagues and epidemics, such as the Black Death, which is estimated to have swept away a quarter of the inhabitants of Europe, or of famines, such as the Russian famine after the War, when whole districts relapsed into cannibalism. One need not be a sentimentalist to echo, as one reads human history, the words of the poet O'Shaughnessy,[10] and say:

> But the floods of the tears meet and gather;
>   The sound of them all grows like thunder:
>   O into what bosom, I wonder,
> Is pour'd the whole sorrow of years?
>   For Eternity only seems keeping
>   Account of the great human weeping:
> May God, then, the Maker and Father—
>   May He find a place for the tears!

Now it can hardly be denied that the extent of human misery everywhere, and in all ages, does constitute a very real difficulty for religious minds. There are, of course, many comfortable, middle-class people who, just because they themselves have always lived sheltered, easy lives, believe that " all is for the best in this best of all possible worlds." But with those who are brought into close contact with life as it is lived by tens of thousands, the matter is far otherwise. I was reading a paper, a few years ago, before a small discussion club, and in the debate that followed a

[9] *Our Mobile Earth*, R. A. Daly.   Scribner, New York, 1926, p. 1.
[10] *The Fountain of Tears*.

Manchester merchant, a man of over sixty, with wide experience of life in Asia and in South America as well as in England, spoke on the subject of Divine providence. I think that, even if I had not known him personally, I should have recognized him at sight for a really good man. But I do know him, and know that he is a man of more than puritan strictness of life, a deeply spiritually-minded man, a man of lofty ideals. But he disclaimed belief in a God of love and goodness with passionate vehemence. The perspiration stood on his forehead, his face went white and his voice shook, as he spoke of what he himself had seen in various countries.

" The dark places of the earth are full of the habitations of cruelty,"[11] was the burden of his speech, and it was clear that the thought of human misery and human wrongs rode his mind like a nightmare. And what parish clergyman is there who is not met again and again by the question : " Can there be a good God while such things happen daily in the world ? " Yet pressing as this problem is, it is not the one that presents the greatest difficulties to the Christian apologist. Human misery can very often be traced to human sin or human folly. And even if the incidence of suffering is very unequal, so that one man sins and another suffers, it is not impossible to put up some defence. After all, we are members one of another, and a world where men and women sinned, but where no one suffered except for his own faults, would certainly be no improvement on the world we know.[12] But what are we to say of the fact, for fact it certainly is, that the whole plan of the animal world, the whole " make-up," so to speak, of the universe, seems bound up with struggle, pain, and death ? " What savagery, what thwartings and delays, what carnage and suffering, what an absence of all that we mean by intelligent planning and oversight, of love, fatherhood ! " Now whereas the thought of " nature red in tooth and claw " was prominent during the latter half of the nineteenth century, it is rather the fashion to-day to dismiss such a view as anthropomorphic exaggeration and morbid sentimentality. Nature's methods,

[11] Ps. lxxiv. 20.
[12] See my book, *The Problem of Evil.* Longmans, 1920, pp. 46–47.

if rough and ready, are not, we are told, really cruel. Animals probably suffer little, and the elimination of the unfit makes for the general progress of the world, for health and strength and beauty. On the other hand, many famous naturalists and men of science have themselves written strongly of the cruelty and ferocity of nature. A very full discussion of the question, giving both sides fairly and dispassionately, is to be found in Professor J. Arthur Thomson's Gifford Lectures for 1915 and 1916, *The System of Animate Nature*, in the chapter entitled "Disharmonies and other Shadows."

For my own part, after giving careful attention to the arguments on both sides of the debate, I have no hesitation in describing the methods of nature as stupid, wasteful, and cruel. Let us very briefly examine the arguments put forward on the other side.

(1) *The lower animals probably feel little pain or fear.* Even if this is true, a point upon which naturalists speak with no sort of agreement and about which certainty is impossible, it is of little weight. The higher animals, and especially men, the highest of all, are capable of intense suffering. Whether insects, fish, and reptiles suffer much or little, *the plan of the universe is such that where suffering is possible it shall be intense*.

(2) *Without such pain and struggle progress would be impossible, and the result of such pain is the progress of the race.* This is by no means universally true. The expression, "the survival of the fittest" deludes many people with the idea that the one that survives is always the one that man would approve on moral, æsthetic, or utilitarian grounds. That, of course, is not true. The fitness involved is *fitness to survive*, nothing more. And the struggle may result in degeneracy as much as in increased efficiency. The ceaseless struggle between the white ants and the true ants has led to the steady degeneracy of the former, not to their increased efficiency. Many parasitic plants and animals, in the struggle for survival, have surrendered literally everything except the power to survive.

(3) *Even if the struggle sometimes results in degeneracy and not in progress, still what progress there has been has resulted from struggle and the elimination of the unfit, and the result as a whole has been good.* But this, even if true, is of no use to the Christian apologist. If God attains ends by means of

pain and suffering, which He could have attained without such pain and suffering, then it would seem that He is not perfectly good. If, on the other hand, God could not attain those ends of goodness, truth, and beauty at which He aims, without pain and suffering, then it would seem that He is not omnipotent.

The existence of struggle, pain, and death in the world seems inconsistent with God's goodness, or His omnipotence, or both.

An attempt is made, from time to time in the world's history, to escape from this dilemma by denying that God is omnipotent. Such an attempt was made, during the moral upheaval due to the War, by Mr. H. G. Wells, who, in *God, the Invisible King*, offered us a non-omnipotent God Who did not create the world, but is evolving with it ; Who is doing His best, and Who in the end may be trusted to overcome all evil, but Who at present comes very far short of omnipotence. Now, of course, no Christian could accept such an idea. The Church has always declared her faith in " God the Father *Almighty, Maker of Heaven and Earth*." And the Church has pinned her faith on a creative, omnipotent God, not from any unreasoning obstinacy, but because experience has taught that the idea of a non-omnipotent, non-creative God is what is known in philosophy as an unstable conception. It is impossible to rest in it. You are compelled either to go forward and postulate another God, omnipotent and creative, lying, as it were, behind and beyond the non-omnipotent God, or else to go backwards and rest content with an evolving universe which stands in no need of any God at all. So belief in a non-omnipotent God always issues, as any student of philosophy could have told Mr. Wells before he wrote his book, either in ditheism or atheism, in two gods or in no god at all. Mr. Wells adopted the first alternative and gave us, behind his Invisible King, another Veiled Being of whom, he assures us, we can know nothing, but of whom he nevertheless tells us a great deal. But no serious student of theology could accept this position. Atheism is at any rate intellectually possible. And theism is possible. And trinitarian theism, belief in one God in Whose nature there are eternal distinctions of person, is not only possible, but intellectually

the most satisfactory of faiths. But an unequal partnership
of two gods, one a Veiled Being, unknowable by man, and
one an Invisible King, knowable and evolving *pari passu*
with the universe, is mere nonsense. The Gnostics at their
worst never thought of anything so preposterous.

No, if the struggle and suffering of the world is to be
fairly and squarely faced, and if at the same time the
goodness and omnipotence of God is to be retained, we must
seek the solution of the problem of pain along quite other
lines. And I am myself deeply convinced that there is no
such solution except such as depends on belief in a Fall,
a deep-seated corruption of the entire universe *ab initio*.
The belief which was almost universal five-and-twenty years
ago, and which is widely held even to-day, that modern
science renders belief in a Fall impossible, is due to the fact
that most men, whether theologians or men of science,
have never really taken the teachings of Darwin seriously.
They have never fully realized the entire identification
of man with the universe. They go on talking about the
Fall of *Man*, asserting it or denying it. But man is an
integral part of the universe, and what we assert of man we
assert of the universe to just the same extent, and in just
the same way, as we assert of a leaf what we assert of a
tree. If man is a fallen creature, the universe is a fallen
universe. If man is essentially spiritual, the universe is
spiritual. If the universe is mechanical, and capable of a
full explanation in terms of matter alone, man is mechanical
and capable of the same type of explanation. To discuss
the Fall of *Man*, above all to discuss it as something which
either could or could not have happened on this earth, and
at some more or less recent date, say in very late pliocene
or early pleistocene times, is absurd. Either there was no
Fall or it was a corruption of the spiritual principle of
the universe from, and indeed before, the beginning of the
evolutionary process. Before we can discuss the question
whether such a corruption can have taken place, and what
its nature can have been, we must learn more of the true
nature of God, and of Man made in God's image. That will
be our task in Chapters VII and VIII. Let us see, here
and now, how the problem of pain is affected by a belief

that the universe is deeply corrupted, and that not merely men are to be redeemed by Christ, but that " the creation itself also shall be delivered from the bondage of corruption into the liberty of the glory of the children of God."[13]

Let us consider first the question of the alleged cruelty of nature. My father was a keen field naturalist, and from a little boy I was interested in natural history. Some time before I was twelve I found an exceptionally beautiful caterpillar. I placed it in a box, and fed it with the leaves of the plant on which I had found it. In due course it pupated. But when I looked for the chrysalis to produce a rare moth, there came out simply a number of small black flies. Some ichneumon fly had laid her eggs in the living body of the caterpillar, and when the grubs had hatched out, they had eaten out the inside of the still living creature. I can still recall the horror with which I listened to my father's explanation of what had happened, and though I have never lost my taste for reading books on natural history, and for studying nature at first hand as far as my town life has rendered it possible, yet there has, I think, been as much pain as pleasure in the study. Let the reader study any good book on entomology [14] and he will understand what I mean. Now suppose a theologian spoke to an entomologist or marine biologist of this world as created by a God of infinite power and love, what would the man of science reply ? I fancy he would reply : " No, reverend sir, do not say such a thing. You insult my intelligence by such a statement." But suppose the theologian told the entomologist or biologist that God had planned a world " all very good," but that it has been, in some mysterious way, distorted and corrupted ; yet that even now there was a redemptive process at work, steadily undoing the evil, and restoring the good, and making for final perfection. What would the man of science then say ? I can fancy he would reply : " Indeed, reverend sir, I hear you gladly. What you

[13] Rom. viii. 21.   R.V.
[14] For instance : *Problems of Instinct and Intelligence*, by Major R. W. G. Hingston. Arnold, 1928. Or a rather more technical book, *The Social Insects : Their Origin and Evolution*, by Prof. W. M. Wheeler. Kegan Paul, 1928.

say entirely agrees with my daily experience. At one moment I am amazed at the wisdom, power, and beauty displayed in nature, so that I do not know how to find words to express my wonder and love. The next moment J am appalled at the wastefulness, ugliness, cruelty, and stupidity of nature, so that I cry out in a fury, and ask what fiend planned the whole. Yet as I strive to read the record of past ages of evolution, and as I learn more and more of the lessons nature has to teach to-day, I seem to see a redemptive process at work, ever lifting the universe to fresh heights of beauty and of goodness. Do you tell me that God is even now busy restoring a shattered universe? Do you tell me that He will, ' in the dispensation of the fulness of times . . . gather together in one all things in Christ, both which are in Heaven and which are in earth ' ? Ah, reverend sir, I could myself find no better words to describe the process of cosmic evolution. I thank you, from my heart, for your helpful words."

And when we turn from nature to man, from natural history to human history, the signs of God's workings, the marks of this redemptive process, seem to me clearer still. It is often possible to see things—not merely to persuade ourselves that we see them, but really to see them with convincing plainness—when we know that they are there, and are looking for them, though we might have quite failed to notice them if we had not been looking for them. It is so, I think, with God's workings in nature. When we believe in a God of Love, and when we have evidence in our own lives of a process of redemption, it is possible, if not easy, to discern both in nature. I doubt if any one, knowing nothing but nature, would ever have been led to a belief in a God of perfect wisdom and love. For that a revelation was necessary. Christ alone could declare unto us the name,[15] *i.e.* the nature, of the Father ; could, that is to say, reveal God as altogether good, altogether Love. But once we know that truth we can find confirmation of it, dimly perhaps in nature, far, far more clearly in human history. We see both sides of the problem more clearly in human than in natural history. Firstly, we see, with a

[15] John xvii. 26.

distinctness impossible in nature, that sin is the *cause* of suffering. And, secondly, we see that suffering is in itself remedial. If " the blood of the martyrs is the seed of the Church," it is yet more true that the blood, tears, and sweat of saints and heroes and mothers have been the seed from which all good things have sprung. There seem to me to be no words in Holy Scripture more profoundly true and suggestive than the words that " without shedding of blood is no remission of sin."[16]

> Careless seems the great Avenger;
>   history's pages but record
> One death-grapple in the darkness
>   'twixt old systems and the Word ;
> Truth for ever on the scaffold, Wrong
>   for ever on the throne,—
> Yet that scaffold sways the future
>   and, behind the dim unknown,
> Standeth God within the shadow
>   keeping watch above His own.

Often we can see clearly how pain and suffering help to redeem a world, and how the willing sufferer is not only a martyr, but himself also a redeemer. Is it not possible that, as James Hinton teaches in his lovely little book *The Mystery of Pain*, all pain and suffering are remedial, and that even unwilling sufferers do " fill up that which is behind of the afflictions of Christ . . . for His body's sake, which is the Church."[17] If we could once assure ourselves of this much of the sting of suffering would be taken out of it. For it is the apparent uselessness and aimlessness of pain which makes it often so hard to bear.

If then we believe that the universe is not as God willed it to be, but that rather it has undergone some process of corruption and dislocation ; and if, when we come to examine the Fall, we find it to be of a nature in no wise incompatible with either God's power or His goodness ; and if we see,

[16] Heb. ix. 22.
[17] Not, of course, as Lightfoot points out *in loc.*, adding anything to the " full, perfect, and sufficient sacrifice, oblation, and satisfaction of Christ."

F

in the strivings and sufferings alike of nature and of man, a redemptive process ; and if, finally, we believe that God Himself does not stand aside in this redemptive work, but rather Himself takes the chief part, since " He was wounded for our transgressions, He was bruised for our iniquities ; the chastisement of our peace was upon Him, and with His stripes we are healed,"[18] then we shall be able to face the spectacle of a world of sin and of suffering without our courage failing us, without loss of faith in God or of hope for humanity. And surely such an attitude of hope and of courage is a wonderful thing in itself and a wonderful argument in favour of the truth of the Catholic faith. For it is a plain matter of fact that no other religion, no other philosophy, no other way of looking at the world, has anything helpful to say about pain and sin. Often, when I am reading some volume of philosophy, and see how the distinguished writer handles the question of sin and pain, I say to myself : " No doubt all this sounds very convincing in a university lecture-room at Oxford or Cambridge, at Harvard or at Yale. What would it sound like in a slum dwelling in Hoxton or in Walworth, in Hulme or in Salford?" Some time ago a working-man, one of the very finest characters I ever knew, said to me : " Do you know what I did the night before I was married ? I went down on my knees and prayed I might never make any woman as miserable as father made my mother." And then I turn to F. H. Bradley's *Appearance and Reality* and read, in the chapter on *Evil* : " All that we need understand here is that ' Heaven's design,' if we may speak so, can realize itself as effectively in ' Catiline or Borgia ' as in the scrupulous or innocent. For the higher end is supermoral, and our moral end here has been confined, and is, therefore, incomplete. As before with physical evil, the discord as such disappears, if the harmony is made wide enough."[19] A very noble young fellow was looking one day at the photograph of my father, on my mantelpiece. He said : " Is that your father, sir ? It must be funny to have a father you can respect. Mine had never been anything but a curse to us all ever since I can remember." Yet the

[18] Isaiah liii. 5.   [19] *Loc. cit.*, p. 202.

late Professor McTaggart, reviewing the opinions of his brother philosophers, can write : " It has been asserted that the universe, when looked at rightly, may be completely good. Sometimes the standard is challenged, and it is suggested that pain and sin are really good, though we think them evil. Sometimes our comprehension of the facts is challenged ; it is admitted that pain and sin, if they existed, would be bad, but it is maintained that they do not really exist."[20] Only Christianity enables a man to " see life steadily and to see it whole," to face the facts of pain and sin, and to believe in the ultimate triumph of good.

Of course the considerations which help us with the general problem of evil do not enable us to deal fully with the individual case. We may, when we have discussed the question of the Fall more fully, be able to see that natural evils are not incapable of being reconciled with the goodness of God, and yet be unable to say why this particular woman dies slowly of cancer. We may see that in a fallen universe overwhelming catastrophes such as earthquakes and volcanic eruptions are not inexplicable, and still we shall find no answer to the question why this town is over-whelmed and that one escapes. But here the witness which direct apprehension of God yields of His goodness, and that sense of His intimate personal providence and care for each one of us (" I know thee by name, and thou hast also found grace in my sight "[21]), come to our aid. That there should be sin and pain in the world presents no insuperable moral or intellectual problem. That I myself should be tempted, or suffer long continued pain, is a fact best met by reliance on the experimental knowledge that I have that He is Love. That knowledge should help us to say : " Though He slay me, yet will I trust in Him,"[22] and to ask with assured confidence : " Shall not the Judge of all the earth do right ? "[23]

Before we can tackle the problem of the Fall, asking what it can have been, and what may have been its effects, we must enquire more closely as to the nature of God, and of man made in God's image.

[20] *Some Dogmas of Religion.* Arnold, 1906, p. 209.
[21] Exodus xxxiii. 12. [22] Job xiii. 15. [23] Gen. xviii. 25.

CHAPTER VII

THE DOCTRINE OF GOD

WHEN we treat of the nature of God there are two stages in our enquiry. In the first we deal with theism, and discuss the reasons for belief in a personal God. In the second, driven forward by the many difficulties which meet us when we think of a " solitary God," we consider the doctrine of the Blessed Trinity. For personality as it exists in human beings is an idea which it is almost impossible to apply in the case of a simple, unique Being, Who is also infinite. The easiest way of bringing home this difficulty to the ordinary reader is to quote the saying of Professor J. S. Mackenzie that " if God is Love, a solitary God is impossible." From this many thinkers go on to say that God had to create a universe as an object of His love. Christian theologians can, and need, admit no such necessity. God, as revealed in the Christian religion, is not solitary. He is *personal* ; that is He knows, and chooses, and loves. He is not *a person* ; He is not, that is to say, one among others, and if He is limited (and the creation of man, and the gift to man of free will, constitute such limitation) He is self-limited. And God, we believe, has no need for anything outside His own Being. If He creates a universe, it is out of pure love, free benevolence, and not to satisfy any need.

It is probably true that no " proofs of God's existence " are possible. The only way in which man can prove the existence of anything is to experience it as real. If you have had any direct religious experience the existence of God no more needs demonstration than the existence of the sun in the sky. To the man who has no religious experience the existence of God must always remain a more or less probable hypothesis.

But we may approach the matter from a rather different

angle. We may define God as Ultimate Reality. And then the question will not be : " Can we believe in a God ? " but rather : " What kind of a God must we believe in ? " To this question the Christian religion answers, God is a Spirit, God is Love, God is Almighty, God is Three Persons in a Unity of Being. When we say that God is a Spirit we mean the same as when we say that God is Personal. We mean that the nearest analogy we have to God is the spirit or mind of man. To talk of God as " a power not ourselves which makes for righteousness,"[1] a Life Force, the force behind phenomena, is to fall into one of the commonest and most fatal of mistakes, the mistake of trying to explain the greater by the less. If man is conscious, the source of all nature, and so the source of man, cannot be unconscious. An unconscious force, blind power, is less than man ; and God cannot be less than man. God must be personal, and more than personal.

When we say that God is Love we name His chief attribute. But we can also say God is Beauty, God is Wisdom, God is Power, God is Holiness, for all beauty, wisdom, power, and holiness in the world are but rays from Him, the central Sun. In this world we see the beauty, wisdom, power, and holiness of God as we might see a beautiful face reflected in a dull, cracked, uneven mirror. We see it, that is to say, still beautiful and to be adored, but distorted, marred, and indistinct. The subject of God's Almighty power needs rather fuller treatment. Consider the following passage from the chapter entitled " God as Omnipotent " in the late Professor McTaggart's book *Some Dogmas of Religion*.[2]

" When popular theology is pressed to reconcile the present existence of evil with the goodness of God, then it pleads that omnipotent does not mean omnipotent, but only very powerful. But when the sceptic has been crushed, and what is wanted is a belief in the future extinction of evil, then omnipotence slides back into its strict meaning, and it is triumphantly asserted that the cause which has an omnipotent God on its side must certainly win. The confusion is unintentional, no doubt, but it is dangerous."

[1] Matthew Arnold. [2] *Loc. cit.*, p. 219.

This, of course, is pure nonsense. There have been fools among theologians, as among all classes of men, but not all theologians are fools. On the contrary, theology has engaged the attention of many of the finest and most acute minds in every generation. It is not likely that theologians as a class would have fallen into so obvious a confusion. How comes it then that a thinker like Professor McTaggart, usually one of the most clear and accurate of reasoners, should write such a sentence ? It is because he starts with a quite impossible definition of omnipotence. He claims that since " omnipotent " means " able to do all things," God must be able to " create a man who was not a man, or that He could create a being who was neither man nor not man," and if not then " He is not omnipotent." But what are the results of such a way of defining omnipotence ? Two results are at once obvious. They are (i) *God ceases to be a possible object of human thought or speech.* For the possibility of significant thought or speech depends on the *Law of Contradiction* being always valid. If I say : " I am, at this minute, present in my study," the statement has no significance, but is a mere empty collocation of noises unless it excludes the possibility that the statement : " I am, at this minute, absent from my study," should be true. If I say : " Alfred is older than John," I have used words which have no meaning at all unless they mean " John is not older than Alfred." Hence to define Divine omnipotence as Professor McTaggart does is to render all theology impossible, since no statement about God could be either true or false. (ii) *God ceases to have any nature or character whatever.* But the mischief of Professor McTaggart goes deeper yet. A God omnipotent in the sense that he suggests could have no character at all. He could not be a God of Truth, for that means that it was " impossible for God to lie."[3] He could not be a God of Love, since that would imply that it was impossible for Him to be a God of Hate. In short, God could have no character or qualities, since any character or quality would make its opposite impossible for God.

Surely a definition of omnipotence which renders all

[3] Heb. vi. 18.

theology meaningless, and robs God of all attributes, must be wrong. But we can expose the impossibility of Professor McTaggart's definition of omnipotence more clearly still. Let us put a question to him. "Can an omnipotent God be at the same time omnipotent and non-omnipotent?"

If the Professor says No, he has destroyed his own definition of omnipotence, since here is something that an omnipotent God cannot do.

If he says Yes, he lands himself in the statement that in order to be really omnipotent God must also not be omnipotent. Which is mere nonsense.

The truth of the matter is that the Professor has for once fallen into one of a whole class of verbal traps. We have all, I suppose, as children, been puzzled by the question: "What happens if an irresistible force is brought to bear on an immovable rock?" The answer, of course, is that the question is meaningless, since if any rock is immovable, no force can be irresistible; and if any force is irresistible, no rock is immovable. Similarly, Professor McTaggart's definition of an omnipotent being is really no more or less than this: "An omnipotent being is one who can do what can't be done." And so he has no difficulty in showing that the idea of omnipotence is absurd. Now, merely as a point in etymology it may be true that if there is anything that can't be done there can be no such thing as omnipotence. But we do not allow etymology to limit our use of words in this way. Omnipotence is a useful conception, and as long as we define it carefully we are justified in using it in theology. For every science is entitled to *define the sense in which it uses its terms*. How then shall we define God's omnipotence? One obvious definition would be to say that an omnipotent God can do all things that do not involve a contradiction. Thus even an omnipotent God could not both create and not create a universe. And to say this is not in any way to detract from God's glory. He would not be more, but less, divine for being able to contradict Himself. Being a God of Wisdom it is true in the intellectual as well as in the moral sphere that "God is not the author of confusion, but of peace."[4] Of course it is not always possible to say what

[4] I Cor. xiv. 33.

actions do really involve a contradiction. Professor McTaggart instances, as one of the things that he, as a mere man, cannot do, the drawing of a triangle with two right angles. But on a curved surface it is possible to draw an infinite number of triangles with two right angles. or, indeed, with three. Yet I should myself be inclined to say that on a plane surface even God Himself could not draw a triangle with two right angles. For that would be to introduce confusion into the scheme of things of which He is Himself the author.[5] But of one thing we may be sure. God cannot contradict Himself ; He cannot, that is to say, do anything which involves a contradiction.

This suggests an alternative, and I think preferable, form for our definition. I would define an omnipotent being as one whose actions are determined by nothing but his own nature. For the things which are impossible for God, though He is omnipotent in the noblest sense of the word, are not merely those which involve an intellectual contradiction and confusion. If it is impossible for the Source of all wisdom and truth to be the Author of confusion and contradiction, it is equally impossible for the Source of all goodness to be the Author of moral confusion and wickedness, and for the Source of all beauty to be the Author of æsthetic confusion and ugliness. God, as we have already seen, is perfect Love, Wisdom, Holiness, and Beauty, and nothing is impossible for Him except such actions as are a contradiction of His own nature.

So far we have been dealing only with the doctrines of theism. But there are insuperable difficulties in the way of believing in a solitary God at once Personal, Almighty, and Infinite. I have criticised Professor McTaggart's views on God's omnipotence. Yet he was a most profound and stimulating teacher, and I am not sure that there is any man from whom I have received more help. Yet when

[5] Whether the " law of nature," which makes it impossible to draw a triangle on a plane surface, the sum of whose angles is either more or less than two right angles, is itself anything more than another convention analogous to the " great law " that there are always three feet to a yard we need not discuss. One *definition* of a plane surface may be a surface on which the sum of the angles of all triangles is equal to two right angles.

reading his books, and especially his first two, *Studies in Hegelian Dialectic* and *Studies in Hegelian Cosmology*, I have always wondered how he avoided being an orthodox Christian. His first book leads to a position, as to the nature of final reality, which seems to me indistinguishable from rigidly orthodox Trinitarianism. And many of the difficulties in ordinary theism which he discusses in his second book, and in *Some Dogmas of Religion*, vanish at once when we get rid of the idea of a single infinite Person, and accept the Christian doctrine of God. But he was never able to accept—I doubt if he ever really understood—the teaching of the Church, and so he fell away into a profoundly religious atheism, in which the ultimate reality was conceived as being the sum total of human souls. Let us then try to get some clear idea of the Church's teaching as to the nature of God.

In considering the doctrine of the Blessed Trinity there are three things to be noted at the very beginning.

(1) First, the doctrine is not one which man could have found out for himself, by the exercise of his reason alone, apart from the revelation of God ; nor, now that it has been revealed, can it be proved true by logical argument alone. It can be shown to be in agreement with reason, so that a philosopher, or man of science, can believe it without any disloyalty to truth, and without doing any violence to his intellect. But it cannot be proved by reason, so as to be obviously and necessarily true, quite apart from revelation.

Christians, so far from being ashamed of this fact, or unwilling to own it, should be proud of it, and should press it upon the attention of all with whom they discuss religious topics. If the Church had nothing to teach her children which men could not have found out for themselves, by the use of their own intelligence alone, Christianity would be a " natural " religion, and not, as it is, a " revealed " religion. But the Church has much to teach the world which man could never have found out for himself, though when it is shown to him he recognizes that it is true and helpful.

If we ask, " How comes the Church with this special knowledge ? What are the sources of her facts ? " the answer is not difficult. She has two sources of such knowledge. One is, in the facts of the life of Jesus Christ, his Person and teaching. For "no man . . . knoweth the Father, save the Son, and he to whomsoever the Son will reveal Him."[6] The other is, in the constant guidance of God the Holy Spirit, helping her to understand those facts, and to make a right use of them. For our Lord promised that " when He, the Spirit of Truth, is come, He will guide you into all truth."[7]

A man may say : " I do not want, and will not accept, this revealed religion ; I will believe nothing that I cannot find out for myself by my own unaided intelligence." But in every age, and in every country, the wisest and best of the heathen have always earnestly desired that God would reveal himself to man, and have even complained that he did not do so. Surely when the claim is made that God has, as a matter of fact, so revealed Himself to His children, the wise and truth-loving man will say : " This is a claim that I must examine carefully, patiently, and reverently."

(2) Secondly, we must not expect the doctrine of the Blessed Trinity to be simple and easy. We have a perfect right to ask that the Church shall state the doctrine as plainly as possible, so that every man may know what it is that the Church teaches, and what he himself is expected to believe. But we have no right to expect that the nature of God will prove an easy and simple thing to understand, to be grasped by any and every man without effort.

Some time ago a critic of religion wrote : " For goodness' sake do not trouble me with theological puzzles. The religion I accept must be something quite simple and easy." But what answer would be given to a boy who should walk into a night-school and say to the teacher of chemistry, " For goodness' sake do not trouble me with chemical formulæ, and talk about atoms and molecular weights. The chemistry I accept must be quite simple and easy ? " Would he not be told that there was no room for him in that night-school, and that till he approached the subject in a humble and teachable spirit he had better stay away ?

(3) The last sentence suggests our third consideration. While it is certainly not true that all unbelievers are bad

[6] Matt. xi. 27.   [7] John xvi. 13.

men—for there are many causes for an inability to believe, and many very good and noble men have been sceptics—it is equally certain that a bad, careless, vicious life is a very real and a very frequent cause of unbelief. For psychologists tell us that it is impossible to learn anything in which we have no interest. But a careless, indifferent, or vicious man cannot be really interested in God. So if we want to make progress in understanding religion we must strive to live it. That is to say, we must try to be good. For the text St. John vii. 17 should be translated: "If any man sets his heart to do His will, he shall know the doctrine, whether it be of God."

Keeping these three considerations in mind we may now go on to study the doctrine of the blessed Trinity. We must examine: (i) the history of the doctrine, (ii) the meaning of the doctrine, and (iii) the arguments for its truth and value.

If we ask how the Church came to accept this doctrine, the answer is very simple. The early Church inherited from the Jews an intense belief that God is one, and this belief was constantly strengthened and deepened by study of the Old Testament, and by horror at the shameful wickedness and childish folly of the polytheistic heathen religions of the Roman Empire. It is impossible to read the early Fathers of the Church without recognizing the horror and contempt they show for the worship of the many and false gods of the heathen.

But at the same time Christians had the plain words of the New Testament to prove: (a) that Jesus claimed a position, and an authority, which it would have been blasphemy to have claimed if He were not God; and (b) that the New Testament writers used language of Jesus Christ which they could not have used unless they had thought of Jesus as indeed "over all, God blessed for ever."[8] Let any candid man read the New Testament, stopping and asking himself from time to time: "Could Jesus have spoken thus unless he claimed to be divine?" and "Could the writer have used such words of Jesus unless he himself believed that Jesus was God?" and he will be

[8] Rom. ix. 5.

forced to answer both questions in the negative. And the spiritual experience of the early Christians, as of all Christians in all ages, bore out and supported these claims. When they knew Jesus they knew Him as God.

But exactly the same is true of God the Holy Ghost. The early Christians felt, as Christians have always felt and still feel, that the Holy Spirit Who dwelt in them, teaching them, guiding them, and inspiring them to newness of life, was no vague influence or feeling, but a Personal Being, Whom they could know, and between Whom and their souls there could be real intercourse. And when they turned to the New Testament they found that it was as a " Person " that Jesus had spoken of the Holy Spirit, describing His active working as guide, teacher, and inspirer of the Church. And all writers of the New Testament use similar language.

So the early Church was forced to believe the two facts, that God is one, and that the Father is God, the Son God, and the Holy Ghost God. But this is precisely the doctrine of the Blessed Trinity. It is firmly based on the teaching of Holy Scripture, and on the witness of Christian experience in all ages. The Church must hold both sides of the doctrine. In loyalty to Holy Scripture and in loyalty to her own spiritual experience she dare not give up either side of the truth. Both statements must be true, both must be taught and believed.

Down to the time of the great Council of Nicæa in A.D. 325 the Church was struggling to find suitable language in which to express her faith in the unity of the Godhead and the reality and distinctness of the Persons. Sometimes, in laying stress on the unity, some Christian writers seemed in danger of forgetting the distinctions of Person. Sometimes, in emphasizing the reality of Christ's divinity, or the personality of the Holy Ghost, some of them seemed to be in danger of falling into tritheism, the heresy, that is to say, of teaching belief in three Gods. But always the guidance of the Holy Spirit kept the Church in the right path, and helped her to choose the right words and phrases in which to express her faith.

Indeed, it is impossible to read the history of the first four or five centuries of Christianity without an ever-deepening sense of how God has guided His Church. Again and again it would have been so easy—one might almost say so natural—to have accepted the wrong expression. Yet now, looking back over the centuries, we can see how the seemingly harmless expressions which the Church refused to accept would have robbed the faith of all power and life, whereas the expressions she was guided to accept were perfectly fitted to preserve " the faith . . once delivered unto the saints."[9]

Critics of Christianity sometimes speak as if the long struggles of the early Church to win a scientific expression of her faith (for that is what theology is, a scientific statement of the facts of religious experience) were a proof that the doctrine of the Blessed Trinity was not part of the faith of the Primitive Church. It would be just as sensible to say that the solar system had no existence till Copernicus, Kepler, and Newton taught men how to explain the movements of the sun, moon, and planets. The movements of the heavenly bodies were the facts for which men of science had to find a coherent expression. The unity of God, the deity of Jesus Christ, and the personality of the Holy Spirit are the facts for which the great theologians of the early Church had to find a coherent expression. They accepted, and we accept, the doctrine of the Blessed Trinity because it is a full, perfect, and adequate expression of the facts. It adds nothing to the faith set forth in the New Testament ; and if St. Paul and St. John and St. Peter came back to earth to-day, we may be sure they would say of our creeds : " Yes, those words express very clearly and simply what we believed and taught."

What then exactly does the doctrine mean ? Men often say : " How can three Persons be one God ? " Let us suppose that there were a being, some kind of angel, or visitor from the planet Mars, who had never seen anything alive. How difficult he would find it to understand the fact of growth. He would easily understand how a thing can increase, so to speak, from outside, as a pile of stones becomes larger and larger as more stones are thrown on to it. But he would find it hard to understand how anything

[9] Jude 3.

could grow, so to speak, from inside, and by itself. The idea of growth would be to him a thing very hard to grasp. And if he were conceited, impatient, and unteachable, he would almost certainly fail altogether to understand it.

Now let us suppose that this same strange being, having learned something about life and growth, as displayed in trees and plants, were introduced to a new fact, namely, that of intelligence, as displayed in the higher animals. How difficult he would find it to understand what is meant by liking and disliking, choosing and refusing, knowing or being ignorant. If life is hard to understand, how much more difficult is mind. Here, too, he would need to be humble, patient, and teachable if he were to grasp these ideas. But as soon as he began to understand what is meant by mind and how it works, he would have to try to understand something higher than mind, as we find it in animals ; he would have to consider personality, as found in human beings. Here again he would be confronted by something new, strange, and not to be explained by reference to anything with which he had hitherto met. He would have to be careful, humble, and teachable.

Yet two things he ought to have learned by now, namely, that existence is known to us at various levels, as matter, life, consciousness, personality ; and that many of the mistakes in men's thinking are due to the effort to explain the higher by the lower.[10]

He then, our angel or visitor from Mars, will expect, and we, too, shall do well to expect, that when we pass from considering the nature of man to considering the nature of God we shall find something new. We can contrast the nature of man and the nature of God as follows :

The Nature of Man.—The human race, as we know it by experience, consists of an infinite number of minds or persons, each of which is separated from all other minds, and shut up within the circle of its own identity so that one

---

[10] For instance, in the discussions about Free Will, which were in fashion five-and-twenty years ago, it was the habit of unbelievers to compare a man with a gun, or a watch, or a pair of boots. All such comparisons were absurd. You cannot adequately compare a mind with a thing.

mind cannot ordinarily share the thoughts, feelings, and desires of other minds except by means of the medium of speech.[11] And secondly, in each mind or person only a part of human nature is displayed, so that " it takes all sorts to make a world."

The Nature of God.—The Godhead, as we know it by revelation, consists of three minds or Persons, each of whom is perfectly one with the others, sharing every act of knowledge, love, and will, so that there is no barrier of individuality between the Persons. And secondly, in each person the entire nature of God is displayed, so that " we are compelled by the Christian verity to acknowledge every Person by Himself to be God and Lord " (*Athanasian Creed*).

We can get a faint picture of this life of God in the following way. Every one must have noticed how, when a man and a woman have lived together in perfect love for many years, they seem hardly to need to speak. They have become so closely united in thought and will and desire that the barrier between the one soul and the other seems to have been broken down. If we imagine that love heightened a million times, so that the oneness, the unity, likewise is deepened a millionfold, we get some faint picture of the perfect unity of the three Persons in the Blessed Trinity.

Does not the doctrine of the Blessed Trinity, as here stated, go dangerously near to tritheism, or a belief in three Gods ? No, for we do not believe in three Persons all of Whom are independent and self-existing. That has never been the doctrine of the Church. The Father alone is self-existing ; that is to say, He alone exists through His own power. The other two Persons are derived and draw their life from the Father. " The Father hath life in Himself " ; He has " given to the Son to have life in Himself."[12] And we say of the Holy Spirit that He " proceedeth (that is, draws His life from) the Father and the Son."[13]

[11] This isolation and loneliness of each mind or person is a frequent topic among poets. The reader should read Matthew Arnold's *Isolation* (*Poems of M. Arnold*, World's Classics, p. 121), or Lord Houghton's *Strangers Yet* (*Golden Treasury of Songs and Lyrics, Second Series*, p. 88), or Francis Thompson's *A Fallen Yew* (*Selected Poems*, p. 48). But the idea is common to many poets and thinkers.
[12] St John v. 26.   [13] *Nicene Creed* : compare St John xv. 26, xvi. 7.

Here again, if we are careful to remember that comparisons and analogies are poor and weak in such cases, we may think of God the Father as an eternally burning light, and of God the Son as the reflection of that light in a mirror,[14] and of the Holy Spirit as the radiance streaming out from the light and from its reflection in the mirror. But such an analogy must not make us forget that we believe in three divine Persons, not in one Person acting in three different ways. For that is not the Christian faith revealed by God.

The strongest argument for the truth of the doctrine of the Blessed Trinity is that it alone is adequate to meet the facts of Holy Scripture and religious experience. After centuries of discussion no other form of words could be found which would give expression to all sides of the truth.

But there are many things which confirm our faith in it. This doctrine which was accepted, not in obedience to the teaching of philosophers, but, as it were, in their very teeth, and was indeed " hid from the wise and prudent and . . . revealed unto babes,"[15] has, in the centuries that have passed since the Council of Nicæa, received wonderful support. Many different lines of human experience and human thinking lead up to, and find their fulfilment and explanation in, this doctrine. We can only notice one or two ; thus :

(1) *Mysticism.*—All the great mystics, especially the most original and independent, as Plotinus the Greek mystic, Eckhart and Boehme the Germans, and some of the Sufi (Mohammedan) mystics, who have claimed first-hand experience of the nature of God, have taught a doctrine of spirit which strangely supports the Christian doctrine of the Blessed Trinity. They have taught, that is to say, that man can lose the restraints and limitations of merely individual existence, and be absorbed in and united to God, yet without loss of personality. In the Buddhist Nirvana the soul is reabsorbed into nothingness, and lost as a drop of rain is lost when it falls into the ocean. But this is a gloomy faith. The mystics, taught by their own first-hand experience of God, know that the real nature of Spirit is such that complete surrender of the isolated life of mere

[14] Compare Heb. i. 3.   [15] St Matt. xi. 25.

individuality, and complete union with God, is not incompatible with the retention of distinctions of personality. It is only such a conception of the true nature of Spirit as is revealed to us in the doctrine of the Blessed Trinity, and such as is foreshadowed in the prayer : " That they all may be one ; as Thou, Father, art in Me, and I in Thee, that they also may be one in us,"[16] that explains the mystic's experience of God.

(2) *Philosophy.*—The result of twenty-five centuries of philosophy might almost be summed up by saying that a philosopher can neither give up belief in separate and immortal souls (that is, in the doctrine of personality) nor retain a belief in distinct individuals wholly separate from each other without falling into confusion and contradiction. If, remembering that man was created in the image of God, he accepts the Church's doctrine of the Blessed Trinity as his guide to the true nature of man, he gains clear guidance at once.

(3) In *Ethics*, the science of right and wrong, and in *Sociology*, the science of society, the idea of a community life, in which the life of mere individuality is absorbed into, but not lost in, a higher unity, becomes daily of greater importance.

(4) *Mathematicians*, in studying the idea of infinity, quite apart from the idea of an infinite God, have been led to a doctrine of the infinite which strangely reflects the Church's doctrine of the Blessed Trinity.

For the modern conception of the " infinite " in mathematics involves the view that if anything is infinite the whole will be perfectly mirrored in its parts ; and also that if any whole is of such a nature that it is perfectly mirrored in its parts then it is itself infinite. Let me take two very simple illustrations :

(1) Think of the series of all whole numbers from one to infinity. Thus :

Series A.—1, 2, 3, 4, 5, 6, 7, 8, 9, 10, 11, 12 . . . ∝

This is an example of what is called an infinite series. Now pick out each third term and write them :

Series B.—3, 6, 9, 12, 15, 18, 21, 24, 27, 30 . . . ∝

[16] John xvii. 21.

G

This series is obviously only a portion of the first series.
Yet it can be written :

$$3 \left\{ 1, 2, 3, 4, 5, 6, 7, 8, 9, 10 \ldots \propto \right.$$

which gives us the original Series A multiplied by 3. Which
looks as if Series B was at once a third of Series A and three
times Series A. This, of course, would be an incorrect
way of putting it since each series is infinite, and each is
an infinity of the same order. But we can say that because
the Series A is infinite it is perfectly mirrored in its parts.

So when the atheist, on Woodhouse Moor, Leeds, was
ridiculing the doctrine of the Blessed Trinity, and ex-
claimed : " When my little girl of six goes to Day School,
on a week-day, they teach her that three times one are three ;
but when she goes to Sunday School, on a Sunday, they
teach her that three times one is one. Which is right ? "
the proper answer would have been : " Little girls of six
can't be expected to know everything. If she grows up, and
goes to college, she will know that you are talking nonsense."

Here is another illustration. A boy wears a button in
his buttonhole, and on that button there is a perfect photograph of himself. But if it is a perfect photograph of himself it must *show him wearing a portrait button.* But the
button shown in this portrait must itself have on it *a
portrait of the boy wearing a portrait button.* The reader
probably knows the rhyme :

> Big fleas have little fleas
> Upon their backs to bite 'em ;
> And little fleas have lesser fleas
> And so on *ad infinitum.*

So the series of pictures on the button grow smaller and
smaller *ad infinitum.* Because the first photograph on the
button is a true and perfect picture of the boy wearing the
button the series must be infinite.

If this is indeed a necessary property of the infinite,
namely that the whole should be perfectly mirrored in its
parts, we need not wonder that in God, Who is infinite,

Being is of such a character that, as we have seen, the entire nature of God is displayed in each Person of the Blessed Trinity ; so that " we are compelled by the Christian verity to acknowledge every Person by Himself to be God and Lord."

CHAPTER VIII

GOD, MAN, AND THE UNIVERSE

WHAT all thinking men and women need in these days is a mental picture of reality, of God, Man, and the Universe, and of the mutual relations of the one to the other. They need what the Germans call a *weltanschauung*, a world-view which finds room for all their beliefs, religious and secular, moral, artistic, and practical. The early Christians had such a mental picture, as we learn from 2 Peter iii. 5-7, where, in three short verses, the writer sketches the origin, nature, and destiny of the universe as he conceived of it. That view was deficient in many respects from the point of view of modern physical science. But it was coherent, and adequate to the mental and moral needs of the time.

The passage quoted in Chapter III, where Archbishop Temple says : " In the flower of the Middle Ages philosophers had achieved a systematic unity of existing knowledge, under the reign of theology, the Queen of the Sciences, such as has never been repeated," witnesses to the fact that men in the Middle Ages had such a *weltanschauung* as they could live by. The man of the present day has no such unified mental outlook. Thinking, as most people do, rather in mental pictures than in abstract concepts, he uses religious pictures which his grandparents were already finding a little old-fashioned, and alongside of them pictures of the physical universe which, if much more modern, are none the less out of date owing to the rapidity with which scientific hypotheses and theories change and give place to newer ones.[1] He is like a man trying to put together, into one coherent picture, pieces of half a dozen different jig-saw

[1] A recent writer, in a scientific magazine, said : " Anything published to-day about the Quantum Theory runs the risk of being out of date before it is in print."

puzzles. If we add to these difficulties the break up of old
moral standards due to the War, and the profound social
unrest springing from the same cause, we need not wonder
if men and women fail to find rest for their souls. For there
are few sillier things that any man has ever said than the oft-
repeated saying that it does not matter what a man believes
so long as his life is right, since no man's life can be right till
he has a coherent philosophy of life. Much of the restlessness
and unhappiness of youth—and youth, to the thoughtful
and sensitive soul, can be a very unhappy time—is due to
just this, that the various elements of life have not yet been
focussed and harmonized. Now it is the special task of
religion, on its intellectual side, to provide such a harmonized
view of all reality. Let us see if we can sketch, even in the
barest outline, a *weltanschauung* adequate to our day.

We start with God. He is a timeless, self-existing Being,
the sum and source of all Truth, Beauty, Wisdom, Power,
and Holiness. And in that Being there are three centres
of Knowledge, Love, and Will : three Persons. Not three
individuals, nor anything remotely resembling three
individuals. God is One ; but in that one Being there are
three centres of consciousness. When I was writing on this
subject some time ago, in a weekly paper, I received the
following question : " When you used the word ' God,'
without qualification, to whom do you refer ? To God the
Father ? Or to the Blessed Trinity ? " The question is
badly worded, and so is difficult to answer. But as far as
it is possible to answer it I should say that when we speak
of any one of the three Persons, Father, Son, or Holy Spirit,
we do well to speak of Him as God, being " compelled by
the Christian verity to acknowledge every person by Himself to be God and Lord " ; but that when we speak simply
of God " without qualification," we refer to that triune
Being in Whom those distinctions of Person exist. One
difficulty we have, in thinking of the Blessed Trinity, is
due to the fact that we have come (quite naturally, perhaps
inevitably) to think of a multitude of separate, isolated
individuals as the natural form which spirit takes, and as
the only possible form of existence. We must teach ourselves
to recognize *a higher type of being*, "Three in One, and One

in Three." Perhaps we may see reasons for recognizing "Many in One, One in Many" as the true form in which human spirit exists or should exist, and may come to see that the life of spirits shut up each in its own isolated circle of individuality is an unnatural and perverted condition.

Granting then that there are, in God, three centres of Will, as also of Knowledge and of Love, we may legitimately ask : "What holds these three centres of Will, these three Persons, together ? " Three wills may will three different things. Unless we are to empty the word "Will," when applied to God, of all meaning we are forced to ask the question : "How is the unity of God maintained ? " It is, of course, no external or formal unity ; as we might conceive of three human souls in a single body forced to act in union as the condition of being abl eto act at all. It is, equally of course, no internal mechanical unity ; as a machine is a unity, and can only move if the parts act in harmony. No, we may unhesitatingly assert that the unity of the Blessed Trinity is a moral unity, the unity of Love. The late Dr. J. R. Illingworth, one of the most profound thinkers that the Anglican Communion has possessed in the last half century, did not hesitate to write : "We are told that God is Love ; and love, as we know it, must be shown in sacrifice ; though the sacrifice grows painless in proportion as the love is pure. And when we recall how in the days of our Lord's ministry on earth Father, Son, and Holy Spirit bore Their witness each to other, but no one of the Holy Persons ever to Himself, we are led on to wonder whether "in the light that no man can approach unto," where the Three are One, some higher analogue of what we call sacrifice does not for ever flame, whose radiant reflection on the universe only becomes shadow when it falls on a world of sin." [2]

Now no words that man can use, no thoughts that he can think, can picture the richness of the content of the life of this triune God. All the power, wisdom, beauty, and goodness which are displayed so lavishly in the universe

[2] Essay on "The Problem of Pain" in *Lux Mundi.* John Murray, 1889.

are, we believe, but as a drop to the ocean compared with the power, wisdom, beauty, and goodness in God, Who is the source of all. We may well exclaim, with St. Paul : " O the depth of the riches both of the wisdom and knowledge of God ! how unsearchable are His judgments, and His ways past finding out."[3] And the life is perfect and complete in itself. Nothing is lacking to it. Nothing could add anything to it. So the universe was created, not to meet any need of God's, as some modern thinkers vainly suppose, but out of pure love, pure benevolence. God, being pure Love, desired that other conscious beings should share His life of bliss. So God created man.

The writer of the Epistle to the Hebrews says of God that " because He could swear by no greater He sware by Himself."[4] And we may say that because He could take no greater pattern after which to create man, He created him in His own likeness. God is One, and in the unity of the Godhead are Three Persons, centres of consciousness. Unfallen man, I believe, was one, and in the unity of unfallen manhood were all the souls, centres of consciousness, that ever have or ever will exist. Now such a spiritual being implies a universe in and through which it lives, and manifests itself.

Here a short digression is necessary. Nearly all philosophers and men of science are very much opposed to what is known as " vitalism."[5] Now if by the doctrine of vitalism we are meant to understand belief that in every living organism there is a kind of vital fluid which might, at any rate conceivably, be isolated and put up in a bottle, or a kind of vital force which might conceivably be transformed into some other kind of force, say heat or electricity, in accordance with the law of the conservation of energy, then no sane person would wish to defend a doctrine of vitalism. But if by the doctrine of vitalism we mean no more than a denial that, when the actions and reactions of an organism have been adequately described in terms of mechanism or

[3] Rom. xi. 33.   [4] Heb. vi. 13.
[5] But see Prof. Wm. McDougall's *Body and Mind : A History and Defence of Animism.* Methuen, 1911. And *The Science and Philosophy of the Organism*, by Prof. Driesch, Gifford Lectures, 1907-8.

of chemical action, the final word has been said, then all
Christians, and all philosophers who are not pure materialists,
must be vitalists. Even so luminous a thinker as Dr.
D'Arcy, Archbishop of Armagh, whom I have always ranked
among the half-dozen thinkers to whom I owe most, seems
to me to fall into confusion on this point in his little book
Science and Creation.[6] After definitely rejecting belief in
the "need for any Life-Force, Entelechy, or *élan vital*"
(p. 47), he says: "The one principle which can truly
illuminate the darkness is that of a Supreme Universal
Intelligence permeating and controlling the course of
evolution—an intelligence compared with which our greatest
minds are as nothing" (p. 63). This appears to me to mean
God. But how is God to be conceived as acting? Upon
the universe, from without? Then we are landed back in
eighteenth-century deism with all its difficulties and contradictions. Upon the universe, from within? Then we are
perilously near pantheism. Nor am I, when I watch an
ichneumon-fly laying her eggs in a caterpillar, or cancer of
the larynx bringing a man to death by a lingering process
of starvation or suffocation, able to believe that I see God
at work. No! we must approach the whole matter along
other lines. One great difficulty to-day springs from the
fact that, as I have said, few theologians or men of science
take their Darwin seriously. They do not really think of
man as an integral part of the universe. They unconsciously
think as if it were indeed true that

> All the world's a stage,
> And all the men and women merely players.

But the world is not a stage on which human beings, as
distinct from the world, as actors are from the boards they
tread, may come and go. Man is a living part of a living
universe, as a leaf is a living part of a living tree on which
it grows. And the soul of the universe is the spirit of man.
Or, if you like, you can express it the other way and say
that the soul of man is the most highly developed, the most
distinct, part of the spiritual basis of the universe. Let
us see what, exactly, this means.

[6] Longmans, 1925.

Fancy that you have in the palm of your hand a grain of wheat, and a piece of wood carved to look like a grain of wheat, and so well done that it needs examination under a microscope to distinguish them. If you plant them one will give rise to a wheaten plant, complete with root, stalk, leaves, and full ear of corn. The other will give rise to nothing. Why? The only possible answer is that the grain of corn is alive. The life, soul, spirit of the grain of wheat is the true cause of the wheat plant. Then we may say:

The cause of the wheat plant is the life or soul which is in the grain of corn.

The cause of Mr. John Smith's body is the life or soul of Mr. John Smith.

The cause of the universe is the life or soul of the universe.

And that soul of the universe is not, as Goethe taught, God; it is God's created image, man.

When then God created, in His own image, that unity of human souls which, for convenience, we may call Adam (Adam=The man), that spiritual unity necessarily gave rise to an universe.[7] And since the spirit was a single

---

[7] If "Adam," the unity of all human souls, is conceived of in this way, it follows that the number of souls is *great but not infinite*. If the will of God that all men should be saved (1 Tim. ii. 4) is ultimately realized, then the number of souls in Adam, the number of distinct centres of consciousness in the original unity, would be also "the number of God's elect." But if the number of human souls, however great, is *not infinite, but just so many and no more*, then we might expect the universe itself to be, however large, not infinite either in amount of matter or in extent. But this is the view which modern science regards as at least probable. The Hon. Bertrand Russell, in his book *The A B C of Relativity*, writes: "We must therefore suppose that there is some definite number of electrons and protons in the world: theoretically a complete census would be possible" (p. 164). And again later he says: "All arguments as to regions which are too distant to be observed depend upon extending to them the laws which hold in our part of the world. . . . We cannot therefore say that the universe *must* be finite. We can say that it may be, and we can even say a little more than this. We can say that a finite universe fits in better with the laws that hold in the part we know, and that awkward adjustments of the laws have to be made in order to allow the universe to be infinite."

united spirit the universe in and through which the life of that spirit was expressed was " all very good," an universe growing and developing as a single healthy organism, without strife or discord or pain.

But what could hold the unity of human souls together so that it might remain an unity ? We may say of God's created image, man, as we said of God. The unity could only be a moral unity, the only possible bond must be the bond of love. But if the individual souls refused to exercise that mutual self-sacrifice which Dr. Illingworth believed exists even between the persons of the Blessed Trinity, if the individuals asserted themselves against the unity, then the very nature of man would be shattered. Now it is in just such an assertion of the self against the unity that the unknown author of that exquisite little mystical work of the fourteenth century, the *Theologia Germanica*, sees the cause of the Fall. He writes :

" It is said it was because Adam ate the apple that he was lost, or fell. I say it was because of his claiming something of his own, and because of his I, Mine, Me, and the like. Had he eaten seven apples, and yet never claimed anything for his own, he would not have fallen."

And the view of the Fall which I am suggesting is supported by the observed fact that all sin seems to be at root some form of selfishness and self-assertion. I have heard Archbishop Temple say that virtue consists in acting as if every one mattered except yourself, and sin consists in acting as if no one mattered except yourself. But I do not want to advance arguments in favour of this view of the Fall. I have done that elsewhere.[8] Here I merely offer it as a hypothesis, though I shall consider one or two of the objections urged against it a little later.

If the individual souls asserted themselves against the unity, if, that is to say, they chose the life of self rather than the life of love, there are three things which we can say:

(1) A root of discord, sin, and death would be introduced into the universe for which man would be wholly and entirely responsible. None of the responsibility for the sin and

[8] In *The Problem of Evil*, Chapter VII.   Longmans, 1920.

suffering of the world would rest with God. As we have seen, a God of real omnipotence cannot contradict Himself. But to create a free spiritual being who could not choose the selfish life instead of the life of love, if it chose to do so, would be a glaring contradiction. For a free spirit must be able to choose freely. In this connection I cannot forbear quoting again, though I have made full use of it in my earlier book on the subject, an extremely relevant passage from the *Treatise on Divine Names* of the writer who passes under the name of Dionysius the Areopagite. He says :

" Wherefore we will not admit the vain statement of the multitude, who say that Providence ought to lead us to virtue, even against our own will. For to destroy nature is not a function of Providence."

But to *force* free spirits to *choose* good and not evil is a contradiction in terms. If they are forced they do not choose. But to *force* free spirits to *be* good is to destroy their nature as free spirits, and so is no function of Providence. So even for an omnipotent God there would seem to be only the alternatives, when creating a world, of creating free spiritual beings, who *might* continue steadfast in virtue, but who *might* fall, or to create automata, who would always act rightly, like perfect machines, but who would be no fit objects of Divine love. For what earthly parent would hesitate which to choose, a son who might grow up bad but who might be led, by patient love, to a life of virtue, or an ingenious mechanical doll who would perform all its evolutions faultlessly, *of necessity but not of love* ?[9] When God created men He had to give them the liberty of falling if they chose. And when they fell there was, even for Divine omnipotence, only two possible courses :

[9] The point that a free being cannot be *made* to choose is so important that an illustration may be of value. I was once sitting opposite a stout, florid woman in a tram. She was talking to her friend of summer bonnets, and said : " No, my dear, I don't like it. If I had had my way I would have taken the one with the roses. I like a bit of colour myself. But my husband is so difficult. He made me choose this one." But clearly she was wrong. He did not make her *choose* that one. He made her take it. In her heart she still *chose* the gaudy one.

to annihilate the whole race, or by patient love to seek to buy them back (redeem them). The first, being Love, He could not do. The second course, God's plan of redemption, is the key to all history.

(2) The whole universe would be shattered and destroyed by man's fall. Adam, the unfallen unity of all souls, was, we believe, the soul of the unfallen world. But a shattered and broken unity could no more produce a universe than a grain of corn *after it had been ground into flour* could produce a living wheat plant.

(3) There would be, in the scattered fragments of human nature, no power of coming together again, no inherent principle of regeneration. Before the redemptive process could so much as begin it was necessary that the creative Spirit of God should do again what He had already done once, and create a new human nature. We commonly speak of Christ having " taken our nature upon Him." Strictly speaking, this is incorrect. He brought us a new nature. He is the start of a new creation ; He is the Second Adam. And this creation of a new human nature, and the assumption of that nature by the Logos, the Second Person of the Blessed Trinity, was the starting point of the whole cosmic process as we now know it.[10] The whole process of evolution, as modern science reveals it to us, is nothing more than the gathering together in one of all things in Christ, of which St. Paul speaks. Professor Burkitt, in a kind reference to my views in his book *The Religion of the Manichees*,[11] regards them as Manichæan.

[10] The necessity for re-fashioning the whole fallen universe, *i.e.* the spirit of man and visible world which is the organism of that spirit, in the likeness of the Logos, in Whose likeness it was created, is well expressed by S. Anthanasius, in his treatise on the Incarnation, as follows : " For just as when someone's portrait, drawn on a panel, has been rendered invisible by the dirt that has overlaid it, it is necessary for the man whose portrait it is to be present in order that his likeness may be renewed on that same panel—since it is for the sake of the portrait that the panel itself, on which it has been drawn, is not thrown away, but is repainted—so too the all-holy Son of the Father, being the image of the Father, came to our dwelling-place to restore man, created after His own likeness, and by remission of sin to recover him as one lost."

[11] *Loc. cit.*, p. 100.

But Mani regarded the principles of light and darkness as two independent, eternally distinct principles. Such a dualism is impossible to modern minds. Yet sin and suffering continually impress themselves on our attention. What shall we say of them ?

Shall we deny their reality and call them an illusion ? Shall we, with Mani and Bardaisan, believe in two independent spiritual beings eternally at war ? Shall we lay the sin and suffering of the world at God's door ?

Or shall we say that sin and death are the result of man's free choice of the selfish life of individual self-assertion, and will be cured only when all men shall be once more one, one in joyful and free surrender to God, one *in* Christ Jesus ? The world-view which I find satisfying, which finds room for all the teachings of theology, philosophy, and physical science, may be described as follows :

(1) The triune God.

(2) The unity of humanity, the sum of all souls in a unity of being, the first Adam, created in the image of God.

(3) That unity producing, by the natural and inevitable activity of all spirit, a harmonious universe, free from strife and discord.

(4) A Fall, or shattering of that unity of humanity, due to the assertion of the individual souls against the unity ; a disruption which inevitably involved the total disappearance of the universe.

(5) The creation, by the creative Spirit of God, of a new human nature, which was assumed by the Second Person of the Blessed Trinity, Who thus became the Second Adam.

(6) The gathering together of the fragments of the shattered universe *in* Christ, a process which becomes conscious in man. The strife between the old fallen human nature and the new humanity of Christ, between the fallen soul of the universe and the new Soul, the Logos, is the struggle between light and darkness that all serious thinkers, and not the Manichees only, have recognized. And the struggle, on its physical side, is the struggle of cosmic evolution. " The whole creation groaneth and travelleth in pain together."

(7) The final consummation when, the old man being wholly done away, and the new man raised up, there shall be "new heavens and a new earth, wherein dwelleth righteousness."[12]

Two objections are often brought against this doctrine of a pre-cosmic vitiation of the whole life-force, at the very beginning of cosmic evolution. They must be briefly examined.

(1) It is said that such a theory is pure mythology, for which, in the very nature of the case, there can be no evidence. Now any one is at liberty to say that the evidence is insufficient to secure conviction. But to say that there can be no evidence is to go too far. The late Sir George Darwin originated a theory that the moon once formed part of the earth, and has slowly receded further and further from the parent planet. If this occurred at all, it did so before there was life of any kind on our earth. Yet no one would say that there could be no evidence for the theory. It is accepted because it best explains a great number of observed facts. So with the ice ages, which geologists believe to have occurred at various periods in the earth's history. Even if creatures rightly to be classed as human witnessed the last of those glaciations, they left us no record of them, and the earlier ice ages occurred millions of years before man appeared on the earth. Yet no educated man says that the geologists' accounts of ice ages in the past are mere mythology for which no proof can possibly be produced. Men of science believe in such ice ages because of the traces which they have left upon the surface of the rocks. If theologians come to accept belief in a pre-cosmic vitiation of the whole life-force, they will do so because such a hypothesis best explains a great variety of facts, and because of deep-seated traces which such a vitiation has left on human nature. And certainly the evidence for such a pre-cosmic Fall cannot be wholly lacking, or so profound a scholar as Dr. N. P. Williams, Lady Margaret Professor of Divinity at Oxford, would not have adopted the theory in his Bampton Lectures for 1924.[13]

[12] 2 Peter iii. 13.
[13] *The Ideas of the Fall and of Original Sin.* Longmans, 1927.

(2) It is sometimes said that even if we place the origin of the evil in the world in such a pre-cosmic Fall we have only put it one step further back, and are no nearer explaining it. But that is certainly not so. Dr. Temple, Archbishop of York, writes in his book *Christus Veritas* : [14]

" When in the causal regress we arrive at a will, the regress is at an end, and to understand means, not to give a causal explanation, but to sympathise."

This means that we may say that B caused A ; and that C caused B ; and that D caused C ; and so on for any number of steps. But when we say, of any link in the chain, say of M or of Z, " This happened because Mr. Smith chose to do it," there is no further step that you can take. Mr. Smith, as a free spirit, created in the image of God, is himself the adequate cause of what he wills, and behind his will you cannot go. If you go on and ask : " But what made Mr. Smith choose that ? " you are asking a question that has no meaning. Nothing *made him* choose ; for if it had he would not be a free spirit. As a free spirit man is himself an efficient first cause of what he wills. So when you have found the source of evil in the wills of created beings you have traced evil to its source, discovering the " origin of evil," and relieved God of all responsibility.

I will not apologize to my readers for this long, and I fear dull, discussion of the Fall. What the world needs, what in many respects it is ready for, is a great revival of religion. But no revival can come till we are in a position *to think coherently*. That means that we must have such a restatement of the Faith as shall find room for all the treasures of new knowledge accumulated by mankind since the revival of learning. In making such a restatement it is absolutely necessary for our theologians to make up their minds, one way or the other, about the Fall ; for the conception of man as either fallen or not fallen is fundamental to all theology. In accordance with which view you take you decide whether Christianity is or is not a religion of Redemption. I will repeat here what I said in my last book.

[14] Macmillan, 1924, p. 7.

" The persistent refusal of our leading theologians to face the question of the Fall is playing havoc with theology."[15] How can any man expect to preach with conviction to a careless and indifferent world if he is unable, when asked, to give any certain answer to the question : " Do you believe man to be a fallen being, needing a Divine Redeemer, or do you regard man and the universe as needing only time enough in order to become, by a process of natural evolution, all that God desires ? " When we recognize that the task in which God invites us to co-operate with Him is nothing less than the remaking of the entire universe in the likeness in which it was originally created, the likeness of the triune God, we shall be able to preach a gospel of Redemption, and that gospel will have power.

> Thy nature, gracious Lord, impart,
>   Come quickly from above ;
> Write Thy new Name upon my heart,
>   Thy new best Name of Love.

[15] *Our Lord and Saviour*, p. 71.

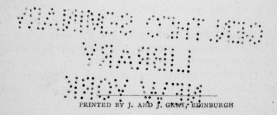

PRINTED BY J. AND J. GRAY, EDINBURGH